Financial Revolution

Matthew A. Easterbrook

INFINITY PUBLISHING

ISBN 978-0-7414-7500-8 Paperback
ISBN 978-0-7414-7502-2 eBook
Library of Congress Control Number: 2012935999

Printed in the United States of America

Published October 2012

INFINITY PUBLISHING

Toll-free (877) BUY BOOK
Local Phone (610) 941-9999
Fax (610) 941-9959
Info@buybooksontheweb.com
www.buybooksontheweb.com

Contents

Contents

CHAPTER 1

Financial Recovery

This book is designed to help the individual consumer fight back against the financial institutions that strive to control all of us on a daily basis. These unscrupulous creditors and corporations are trying to control us and turn people nationwide inside out financially. These financial corporations are taking away our homes, charging us exorbitant fees for using our debit and credit cards, charging us checking-account fees and loan fees, then turning consumers over to collection agencies when we are unable to pay these items and fees. In this time of economic hardship and uncertainty, this book will be a building block for you as a consumer to start working on your own individual *consumer toolbox*. It will help to empower you and your family to take back charge and control of your individual finances and fight back against them. Chapter 1 will help you with this and is designed to assist you with a proven budget. As a matter of fact, my wife, Jan, and I saved over hundreds of dollars a month immediately by designing a budget. If *we* did it, you can, too, as a single family or individual. Yes, unless you have a budget you will not ever be able to take—and be in—charge of your own financial destiny.

So let's discuss the first and most important thing, which is designing that needed and necessary budget. The purpose of the budget is to find out where your hard-earned money is going daily, monthly, and, of course, yearly. I call this "tracking your buck." It's a lot like the concept of literally shaving Abe Lincoln's beard off the penny. Yes this may sound satirical, as it sounds a little bit corny, but this is a true concept that will work in the long run to save you big bucks by focusing on—yes—little pennies. Unless you and your family have developed a budget, you will always be plagued by debt and be credit dead.

Just by simply clipping a few coupons, using reward cards, getting membership at grocery wholesale stores, and using advertisement coupons in newspapers, you will save a bundle. These are huge value savers, and this is your start in tracking down your hard-earned bucks. Also, during the holidays, shop within your means and set an amount that you can afford—again, that is in your individual budget. This way, you are spending what you have along with the individual means to do it without putting gifts and other items on high-interest credit cards, thus overspending yourself out of your house and budget. If you have to, start saving for birthdays and Christmas six to eight months ahead of time.

One method is to put away in a savings account a portion of each paycheck every single payday. This will help you save for vacations, holidays, and any miscellaneous, unexpected bills that may arise. This way, you are going on the vacation when you can afford it and are not running up your credit cards that, in the long run, will break you like a pretzel when you get the bill in the mail. So when you are tempted to buy those new shoes, that suit, or that dress, do not charge any of these items, as some of these shrewd credit card companies will charge up to 29.9 percent interest on that piece of plastic called a credit card.

Think about this concept. Rule number one should be to never ever take out a payday-loan cash advance. These advances can cause a snowball effect on you financially. The cash advance first starts off as a financial Band-Aid, but once you start using them, they put you on the hook and keep you coming back every two weeks or on your payday to keep having to renew them. Once a person starts them, he will have nothing but extreme financial hardship and distress in paying off the cash advance. The problem with these short-term financial solutions are that they turn into long-term problems, as it is very hard to pay them off and get rid of them. They are like bad drugs, and, once addicted, you will have a hard time kicking the habit. The way they work is like this: Say you take out a cash advance for $200 or $300; each payday you must pay them off in full, which now shorts you that amount right off the top. No, it's actually even worse, as you have forgotten they charge around 450 percent interest, so for every $200, your interest is around $50, or for $300, it's around $75. So now you are short $250 on the $200 loan or $375 on the $300 loan. Most people, once they start the cash-advance nightmare, can never stop this vicious cycle. So congratulations—you have now taken on another bill, but an even worse one that will drain your paycheck like a glass of water going down the drain.

What is even worse with cash advances is that most consumers, when they get them, are already in financial trouble, but some go out and have to get another cash advance to cover the loss from the first one. So this in turn takes a $200 cash advance with a $50 interest fee, and when you get another one, that interest doubles, so now you are paying $100 every two weeks on a $200 cash loan. So you can clearly see how the negative ripple effect occurs once you start taking out these loan-shark cash advances.

Believe me, I unfortunately know from firsthand experience all too well, as I have used cash advances myself. One reason was being left with enormous bills from a divorce, and I tried to use cash advances to survive. I realized that financially they were killing me more than even the divorce had and that to regain myself again, I had to pay them off to be able to live and survive. Once the cash advance was paid off, I started to save money again and realized they had been way more of burden on me than they had ever helped. My best way of describing my encounter with the cash advances is that they were a cash-advance *addiction*, and once I stopped the addiction, the pain went away.

So the first step in saving money is to get rid of high-interest bills and loans. Go online and get groupons, savers, and grocery coupons. The Sunday newspaper editions can save you a bundle. Shopping at grocery stores that offer reward-card savings are enormous ways to continue your savings. Also, buying the store-brand items at supermarket chains that offer these rewards are great buck trackers. In fact, my wife and I have found that buying the store-brand items really is not any different than the name-brand products and that they cost sometimes nearly only half the price—or are at least fifty cents to a dollar cheaper per item. We have even found that with bakery items, a lot of them are more fresh and even better than other packaged named brands. My wife, Jan, always cuts out coupons when we go shopping and buys reward-card saving items. Her hard work always pays off at the register when we check out; she saves us big bucks. I can remember on one of our grocery-shopping adventures, Jan having a stack of coupons and using our reward-card savings. Guess how much she saved on this one shopping spree? Okay, give up! Jan was able to save around $52, and instead of our groceries costing $150, they came to around $98. Jan does this every time we go to the supermarket. This in turn always gives us a cushion every single month.

Imagine putting away in a savings account $52 every single month and watching it grow. This definitely is a step in the right direction in improving your monthly budget. The classic term here is "the more you save at the store, the more bucks you have in your pocket and overall budget."

Balancing your budget is not easy and requires extra care and effort on your part. So take action steps, and try to limit how much you drive your car. If using a bus to commute is an option, do it. If not, getting into a carpool or using an Amtrak train are definite steps to improving your budget and improving the environment at the same time. Not to say the least, when gas is sky rocketing at around $4.29 per gallon, using alternative means of travel will save you and your family hundreds of dollars per month. Maybe even go for walks to run errands around town instead of burning gasoline in your car and polluting the environment. These are action steps to saving money. My wife and I walk around town all the time, and it has paid off enormously financially—not to mention we are also in better physical shape, as well.

Okay, here is a saving tip: do not eat out on a regular basis, and avoid junk foods. These bad foods are usually more expensive to purchase and are not a healthy food choice.

Vegetables and fruit are good filler foods when you are hungry for a snack. We eat apples, raw carrot sticks, and strawberries in between meals. Just about any raw vegetable is a good choice for a snack item. Avoiding expensive, greasy, non-nutritional-value food items is not only good for your health but, again, will put those hard-earned savings back into your pocket, because you are not buying and consuming them. This way, also, a healthy budget equals a healthy body.

We coordinate as a family going to the movies and out to dinner as a treat. I will admit, once in a while it is fun to go out with my wife on a date. It is also even more fun when we have saved up for the date and know that spending the money is worked into our budget and that we can afford to have this extra fun. It is important to reward yourself on occasion for diligently saving money by following your budget. This will continue to give you the needed motivation and an outlet to break the rigidity of following your strict budget.

A lot of people drink coffee and eat breakfast out. This is very expensive, and you need to take this budget breaker into serious consideration: you're spending about $1.85 for a cup of coffee and around $1.50 for a pastry item. This is just ridiculous, as you are spending approximately $3.35 every day. If you take this number and then multiply it by seven days, that comes out to $23.45 a week. Then multiply this by four weeks, and that's throwing away $93.80 every single month on your unhealthy coffee-and-pastry breakfast. Again, this is an average, and if you were to multiply it by twelve months, you would have spent approximately $1,125 per year just on coffee and a pastry. You will definitely be saving money every day if you make your own coffee and eat breakfast at home. This will increase your daily, monthly, and yearly budget, thus giving you extra monthly and yearly income. You will also find that drinking coffee out, which is not only a budget "buster," but also when you eliminate the extra, nonessential items, then it is a lot easier to follow and stay on your individual budget. I have found that homemade coffee is usually fresher and designed more to my individual taste anyways. It never fails when I have gone out for coffee that the coffee is either too weak or too strong for me. However, when you make your own, you can buy a blend that is just right for your morning wakeup and satisfaction. Remember: the key to a successful budget is tracking down your bucks.

Here is the key to savings in your budget: eliminating expensive junk foods and eating and drinking out. Also find substitutions any way you can that will save you money. These are the true value savers that will maximize your savings in your budget. I have given you some tools, so now I challenge each and every one of you to try to incorporate this into your budget and life. Try it; you may like it. Don't wait; do it right now. Go get yourself a piece of paper and write down a budget or put it on your computer. Whatever your choice of setting it up does not matter. The whole point here is to develop a budget. Then try this budget you have designed for thirty days, and I guarantee that you will be amazed at the results of tracking down your bucks at the end of the month. Trust me, it will be an eye-opening experience that you will never forget but from which you will benefit and be glad that you did take action.

Good luck on your budget, but start today. There is never a good time to start, so taking immediate action is the best time. This way, you will reap the benefits immediately.

CHAPTER 2

Debt Elimination

Since you have started a budget, you're heading in the right direction. The main focal point today is working on debt elimination. Now this is what we touched upon earlier in chapter 1 about the bad debt such as cash advances. These are "must" items to get rid of. If you have the luxury to borrow money from a family member, then do it. Even if you have to put a little money from your paycheck aside, do it until you are able to pay off the cash advance in full to eliminate it completely and forever. Remember, forever means "never again." So eliminate any and all cash advances if you have them, which hopefully you do not.

The next step is to eliminate the plastic troublemakers in your life called credit cards. What I recommend is for people to have one and only one credit card and to use it for only a family or critical emergency. Maintain a zero balance on the card at all times. Remember, having the credit card is not the problem. The problem is using and abusing it and its level of convenience by having it around as a safety net. Abusing the credit card can have some serious financial ramifications. I have personally known people that use their credit cards to buy groceries and other daily necessities. Let's be real here: this is an absolute "no-no." Unless you are starving to death, this is an absolute "do not use" situation—because once your credit card is maxed out, the credit-card companies own your paycheck. In fact, most Americans make minimal payments every month, and this is definitely where the high interest on them "eats your pocketbook alive."

So let's also explore paying these high-interest credit cards down and off as soon as you possibly are able. Now you will start to see some financial daylight, and you are working the process of financial elimination. Now you as an individual will start experiencing the wonders and blessings of having extra money flowing in with these debt eliminations. Your budget will swing like a pendulum in the right direction, and now your budget is starting to work for you, and credit items are at least in the manageable state at this level.

Okay, an area that I warn people about is credit-card consolidation. Consolidating credit-card debt can work, but please be careful when doing it. If you have to, consolidate credit-card debt into a lower-interest-rate loan and close out the higher-interest cards. This is some small reprieve, but remember, the debt is still there. Even doing this small act of financial reorganization will still save you money, and I call this a "value saver." I always encourage people to make as-large-as-they-can-afford monthly credit-card payments for these reasons listed below:

- The credit cards will eventually get paid off.
- You will end up paying less interest in the long run on those high-interest credit cards.
- The higher payments will put more money back into your planned budget.
- Eventually, by paying more "yes," you will end up eliminating, through payoff, the entire credit-card debt. This process will aid you in getting closer to getting out of debt.

Let's look at another debt eliminator called "paying off the car." Car-loan companies do not want you to do this for some very obvious reasons. First of all, say you originally signed a car-loan agreement for a sixty-month term. Do you know that when that sixty months has expired, you, as the car owner, now have paid almost one and a half times the amount that you originally agreed to pay for the car? Rip off? Yes, indeed; it is one of the worst investments you will ever make in your lifetime. This, friend, is only a rough guide. Depending upon each and every person's personal car-buying situation, it may even be a lot worse than that when they examine the paperwork. So what is the solution to this problem? Don't panic, as help is on the way. This is where you hear about people getting what is called a "financial planner." Believe me, the financial planner will pay for him- or herself and will guide you through hard car-buying processes—and through *all* of your financial decisions. The financial planner works and pays for him- or herself, especially over a long period of time.

"What is the solution to my current high-interest car loan?" Yes, I have an immediate remedy for you, and that is to find a way to pay it off as soon as possible. If you have a wealthy family member, this is the time to ask for assistance. Even offer to pay back your family member at a much lower interest rate; or, if you can convince them, a zero-interest loan would really spark your pocketbook. However, most of us do not have that luxury. A real solution would be to make much larger payments. If you can, double payments or make a payment and a half more than the minimum. Now you are shrinking down the high-interest loan and, in essence, are paying a lower rate and reducing down the overall loan amount. This will for sure speed up the car-payoff process and reduce down that high-interest loan in its entirety. Yes, by following this guide, *you* now own the car outright—not the loan company.

Think about this: now, what you were paying in a car payment is going back into your checking account and is giving you way more financial leverage and more monthly income to go back into that budget that you yourself designed.

Here are some more debt eliminators. Seek out programs that will assist those in need. If you are a lower-income person, you may even qualify for electric-bill programs like the "Care Program." A lot of utility companies will allow reduced payments for those on a fixed income. Every person's situation is different, so you have to talk with them and explore your own options, but the programs are available. Some companies give very substantial discounts, so investigate and really learn to become your own "budget detective." Call the utility companies, and inquire about these programs and special discounts. Believe me, they do bulk business, and so they benefit by just keeping you as a customer.

If all of a sudden you become disabled, develop a health issue, or get hurt at work, some insurances have programs to work with you—such as disability insurance and hardship programs—so do not be afraid to ask them what all of your options are in the long run. It is in their best interest to help you make your payments, and it is much better for them to find a way for you to be able to afford the payment than to not make a payment at all. Keep that in mind when talking with a creditor. I have found that most loan companies and credit-card companies do not want you to know about these programs and keep them hidden because they really do not care if you are having problems; if you pay the minimum payment every month, they own you and will continue to take your money at that high interest. However, on the flip side of this, the golden rainbow is on your side as a consumer. There are hardship programs out there that can even give up to six months of deferred payments at incredibly lower rates and payments than what your original monthly payment was in the first place. A good gauge would be that for every $100, they will probably ask for $30. So on a $200 monthly payment on the hardship program, you would be allowed to pay around $60. Yes—huge savings to help you get back on your own two feet again. See how this works? And by using this formula—congratulations!—you have now given yourself back into your budget $140 every single month.

So, if you are currently having a major hardship, call up your loan specialist right now and investigate your options. This is true consumer empowerment, and yes, the "knowledge is power" rule does apply in this case.

This is truly, as a consumer, what loan companies do not want you to know. So here it is. If you find yourself in a financial predicament with your loan company to where you are unable to make your payments, this is what you can do to them as a consumer. First, remember it will take them a long time for any loan company to take action, as there are steps in place that every creditor has to go through when collecting debts. The Fair Credit Reporting Act does protect us as consumers to a large degree, and these companies know this but do not want you to know it as well. Do not be intimated, and now that you are reading my book, you are empowered. Yes, debt collectors will try and scare you with threats of judgments and reporting you to the credit bureaus. Don't forget, if your credit is already bad, then another report right away will not change a bad credit score. On the flip side, to do a judgment against you takes time, and they know it, but they want you to think it is going to happen right away. These are all scare tactics by the loan companies or collectors. No need to worry, help is on the way. It's called Father Time. The main thing to remember is there is no debtors' prison to lock you up in for not paying them. In the case where collectors or creditors continue to harass you or your family by telephone, take immediate action by getting the first and last names of the collectors as well as their titles and—by all means—what companies they represent. Then, after they hang up, write a letter to their company and turn the table on them, threatening them with legal action for harassing you continuously. Trust me, they will stop the telephone calls in fear of the FCRA (Fair Credit Reporting Act). Also state in your written correspondence to the collector/creditor "do not call back" or you will follow through on your legal action.

If for some reason you get behind by three payments, then, in my opinion, just stop paying them and wait them out. What will then happen is the creditor/collector, usually after 90 to 180 days, will start trying to negotiate a settlement offer with you to settle your loan or credit card for less then the amount owed. You can usually settle these accounts with the creditors for sometimes around 15 to 20 percent of the amount owed. In layman's terms, for every dollar owed, they may try and get you to pay them seventy-five cents on the dollar, and never agree to do that when they will on occasion take as low as fifteen cents or twenty cents on the dollar in a settlement. This just gives you a settlement window to work off of, and ultimately the final choice and decision will always be up to you. Never let them pressure you into any settlement. Believe me these loan collectors and creditors are very crafty and will lie to you to get the account settled. Do not forget the golden rule "there is no debtors' prison." If they are unable to convince you to a settlement, in most cases the account will turn into a charge off, which will affect your credit score to a large part, but that is about the maximum damage they will probably do to you for failing to agree upon a settlement amount. Again, with time and always after seven years, this adverse action will fall off your credit report anyways. Time does heal your credit wounds with your credit score. How do I know this? Because I was just like you; my credit score had dropped to a low 509 credit score, which is horrible. At that point, I was credit dead, and if you are there, you are also credit dead right now. The question is: *will I ever be able to rise from this credit-dead status?* and the answer is yes, there is credit resurrection, but it takes time, patience, and hard work to dig yourself out of the grave that you got yourself buried into. I will discuss this more in detail in chapter 4 (on getting a jump on your credit score). So hang in there, my friend, and just simply keep reading this book, as the answers to your problems are yet to come. Remember, it took a long time to get into debt, and it can take just as long to get out of it, but with proactive measures, you can get yourself out of it a whole lot faster. So getting out of debt is a process, and by using some of my principles contained in this book, you can speed up your credit recovery enormously. I had to do this by trial and error, but you have the tools right at your fingertips. No doubt when you have bad credit, it will take time to clean it up.

How To Settle Delinquent Accounts with Your Creditor

All right, how many of us have had a life-changing event? A bill that is unexpected or more than unexpected, like an emergency or crisis bill? Possibly you may have a surprise higher utility or gas bill, or your landlord raises your rent without notice? Are these fair? Heck no, but this stuff happens all the time. For most Americans in this depressed economy, we cannot endure even one extra bill or payment that puts us over the edge. Unfortunately this is life, and it happens to us all on a regular basis. So what happens when this occurs is that some bill ends up not getting paid, and this is when a creditor starts to call and harass us for not paying. This in turn always aggravates us usually paying bill payers and we say, "Screw them, I am not paying them." In fact they have made us so angry that we say, "I will pay them when hell freezes over." I am sure I am hitting home right now, right? Then what happens is the creditor sends your unpaid account to a collection agency, usually after three or more payments have gone unpaid. Then you are sent letters from them, and most people shred them or throw them away—or both. You may even do this for a year or so, am I right? Then, of course, we all have credit amnesia and forget about ever shredding these bills or collectors letters. Then the real bomb hits when you go to buy that home of your dreams, and this is where that creditor or collector bites you right in your buttocks, and you get denied the home loan because of this adverse action. In fact, the lender that denies you (which is usually a mortgage broker or specialist) points out that you will have to pay this account off before they will ever be able to approve you for a home loan. So what do you do in this hopeless situation? I just want to say I have been in your shoes myself, so you deal with it using the formula below.

Method for dealing with home-loan denial

- Save up 75 percent of the delinquent account's total balance.
- Once money is saved, call the collection agency and find out what the balance is that they have on file for you.
- Tell the collector it's outrageous that they are asking for such a high amount of money in such poor economic times. (Never show your hand. Provide a sob story if needed.) They are not always truthful, so turn the tables on the collector.
- Tell them you are destitute and pending bankruptcy, if needed.
- When you make your first offer, start at fifteen to twenty cents on the dollar to settle the delinquent

account. For example, if you owe $1,000, make a first offer of $150–200 to settle the account in full.

- If the collector declines your offer, which they usually will on your first offer, counteroffer but demand to speak with their manager or supervisor, who can make a final settlement on the account.

Be careful when countering, and never let them dictate to you an amount. Whatever they offer you, go lower, and say "this is my final offer." When the collector agrees to the settlement terms, I recommend to settle the account with the agreed-upon amount if you think it's fair. Any amount below 50 percent settlement, you got a great deal, and even up to sixty cents on the dollar is not bad. Over sixty cents on the dollar, refuse and wait them out for a few more months to get a lower settlement offer on the account. Don't forget: time is not on their side, but you have time to wait them out for a better deal.

- Then, a few months later, counter back with an offer of forty-five to fifty cents on the dollar, and tell them once again that if they turn your offer down, you're walking; it's this amount or nothing. I can almost write a script on this, and if this was a Vegas bet, I would say you would win that they will take your offer 95 percent of the time.
- In most cases, the creditor/collector will accept or counter you back very close to what you offered. If they counter seventy cents on the dollar, counter back at fifty to fifty-five cents on the dollar. Always say, "to close them out, this is my final offer," and stick to that offer. If you do not, they will railroad you into paying a much higher settlement. My golden rule is to get the settlement down to sixty cents or below on the dollar, settle the account out, and pat yourself on your back that you closed out a $1,000 account for 600 or fewer dollars. Ultimately, you saved $400.
- I do not recommend working out a payment plan with any creditor, as this will make them not want to settle your account. Remember, your objective is to settle

out the account. The collector's objective is to get money from you, and if you make payments, he is doing his job. So forget about payments; do not agree to payments ever. In my opinion, it prolongs your ability to settle the account once and for all.

- However, never try to settle through negotiation unless you have the money needed to settle the account in full.

Key Principles and Rules When Dealing with Collectors

Some good principles and rules to keep in mind are that collection agencies buy accounts from loan companies and credit-card companies. The more the collector gets from you, the higher the commission for the collector from the collection agency. Some collectors can make from 35 to 50 percent of the entire settlement they get from you, and when they get top dollar, they get paid a lot at your expense. So always keep in mind, when negotiating a settlement with a collector, that there is always a lot of room to negotiate down the settlement amount. They do not want the consumer to know this as they always try and say a certain amount is all they can accept, and that is a bald-faced lie. Yes, collection-agency collectors will lie to you to get you to pay. They are unscrupulous in a lot of ways, so don't fall for their gimmicks. When you do settle with them, it is okay to ask for time to get the money. I always make them wait five days before my next pay period before electronically paying them by an Automated Clearing House (ACH) transaction. This is easy: they will set up the ACH, and make sure you take that amount off your checkbook, because they will take the money and never set one up unless you have adequate funds in your checking account to cover the settlement amount you have agreed upon. Never, ever bounce a settlement with a collector, as this will null and void your entire settlement agreement. The collection agency could—if they want to be real nasty, which a lot will—even seek a judgment against you for bouncing an electronic ACH check. So just do not bounce a check with any collector, or you will regret that forever. Some collectors are so shrewd that they would probably make their own grandmother empty her piggy bank just to pay them what she owes them. I truly believe that collectors are the lowest form of mankind, and they will beg, borrow, and steal just to get you, the consumer, to pay them.

You will be taught in chapter 4 about credit scores and sending payoff letters to credit bureaus. A good practice is to always send a payoff letter to the credit bureau after thirty days in order to eliminate the negative credit history. Always ask for theses paid off accounts to be deleted or listed as paid in full.

The better and quicker the debt is paid off and entered onto your credit report, the better your credit score will reflect; and, of course, the debt or debts will be eliminated forever—provided, of course, that you do not charge them up again.

By following these listed and taught principles, you are already on your way to financial success and the "path of debt freeness." This does require time, patience, and perseverance, but you can and will do and succeed through this process and regain your life. Also, as you are financially stable, you can self-empower yourself to a less stressful life.

You will feel hope and get closer and closer to a debt-free life that you will be able to maintain. Getting out of debt is like hitting your finger with a hammer. You only do it once or maybe twice, and it's painful, so you say to yourself, "I am not going to do that ever again." Debt is very painful, so never forget the pain it caused you when you *do* become debt free. I can say this honestly. I never will forget that pain, and I never will allow myself to fall into that pain again. If I did it, so can you. Believe me, I was buried alive and credit dead.

Another way to get rid of debt—which is not, in my opinion, the best alternative but is another way to work with the problem—is to consult a credit-counseling agency. They are usually nonprofit organizations that charge fees for services. The credit counselors work with you to help lower down your monthly payments. The counselors also assist you in getting your delinquent accounts current with lower interests with the credit-card companies. Usually a credit card will go from 29 percent through their program down to 6 percent with a reduced payment agreed upon. However, you as a consumer using these services will have to always pay the agency on time. The agency then pays the creditor for you from the escrow account they have set up for you. If you miss a payment or are late, they can drop you from the program. This is really bad, because then the 29 percent card goes back into effect and will again start being reported as being late on your credit report. So beware when using these programs.

Basically, any credit-card company can send you to a collection agency if you fail to pay them. Do not panic, for remember, you can usually settle with them for fifty cents for every dollar owed. By you the consumer knowing this, you now have the edge. In fact, you become "the collector strangler" by fighting back and being a good negotiator with these unscrupulous collectors and their agencies. The key to debt settlement and elimination is that creditors do not want consumers to know that they settle accounts on an hourly and daily basis. Creditors definitely do not want consumers to know this, because the more ignorant you the consumer are, the more they can rip you off and the longer they can do it for with, a lot of times, large payments with high interest for long periods of time.

Now that you know this information, you can help others with financial problems know to stop paying the debt, let it go to collection, and then settle it once and for all. Right now, any collection agency reading this is in denial and will tell people this not true, but it *is* true, and this is what they do for a living. Being a collector literally is like having a job where you can rip people off legally and get away with it. In fact, by people self-empowering and fighting back against them, they will start to lose bucket loads of money. So all collectors and collection agencies want to keep this knowledge a secret forever. They want to keep you ignorant and in belief of their lies.

As the consumer, keep this fact in mind at all times: there is no debtor's prison. So collectors' scare tactics are just what they are: tactics to convince you and manipulate you to pay them—period. So when you are dealing with a collector or agency, use this old sales tactic on them: it is called "give and take away." In other words, make them an offer. Let's use this as an example. Take a $3,000 delinquent account. Offer them around 25 cents on the dollar (so that would be roughly $750). When the collector does not accept your settlement offer, tell them very calmly, "Okay, I will pay another delinquent account that will accept my offer." Then also tell them, "Well, I guess when I have some money again, maybe in a year, I will call you again." Then say good-bye and hang up the telephone. I guarantee you they will respond either in writing or call you right back with a new offer. They will be panicking about having to wait a year and will work something out with you almost 100 percent of the time.

Here are some ways to avoid creditors and keep them from harassing you after you make an offer and they refuse to accept it:

- Give them a PO box for your address. Never give out your home mailing address, where they could serve you with a legal judgment.
- If you move, never give a forwarding address, and allow yourself to fall out of their radar. Make no communication with them.
- Never call them; they will store the telephone number you call from in their company's database.
- Communicate with them only when you have enough money saved up to negotiate a settlement offer that works for you.

I moved three times in a year once, and it took the collection agency years to find me. I only spoke with them when I had the money to pay off the account through settlement. They would really listen to me when I talked, because I would threaten to not pay them for a year if they did not cooperate with me, and it worked every time.

Time is on *your* side, not the agency's side, and they know it. Some creditors, when the collection agency is unsuccessful, will take back the delinquent debt after a six-month period or less and give it to a more aggressive collection agency. So they have to get resolution on a lot of accounts right away. Knowing this principle always take your time in paying them off.

Time will always give you ample opportunity to recover both mentally and financially. Yes, of course your credit score will be affected during these waiting periods. I want to tell you that my low credit score was around 509 and I literally had hit rock financial bottom. Waiting for me and probably for you does not matter, because, like I said before, when you are credit dead with a low FICO score, if they make it lower, does it matter? No, so who cares? It will not matter when you have bad credit; it just stays at bad credit until you take proactive measures. So at this point, paying when you are able is on *your* timetable, not the collection agency's or collector's terms. I actually waited until I had saved up thousands of dollars to put myself in a financial position of settlement negotiations. If I did, believe me, you definitely can; and I did this on my own. You are not alone, and by following these principles that took me months to develop, you are pounding the collection agency with your financial toolbox. Why? Because you know what their game is, and you have called all their bluffs and lies by following the provided materials and knowledge in this book.

Some people may look and speak out that what you are doing by waiting and acting on your terms with these corporate financial giants is rebellious behavior. Yes, of course it is; and that is who we rebels are: consumers who are tired of being ripped off, fired, and taken advantage of—and we the people say "it's going to stop *now*." This is why I respect the "Occupy" movements" nationwide. I endorse their cause fully and support it in every way I can and see fit.

The bottom line is, once you settle debt, eventually your credit score does improve—and I myself am living proof. After seven to ten years, the delinquent debts will start to drop off, and so time is on your financial-destiny side at all times. I want to reiterate that you do not have to take being pushed around by collection agencies, threatening collectors, or even sweet-talking, lying creditors or collectors. These bottoms of the totem, pool-sludge-bottom-feeding, sludge-sucking, back-stabbing agencies and representatives have now been exposed and will be held accountable for their actions.

So, I tell you, *stop paying* them when they make demands on you. Stand up to them and pay them when you feel like it and can afford to pay them off with settlement offers only.

Some business professionals might ask what makes me an expert. My answer to them is: my college education, my personal experience in settling the actual debt itself, and my supervisory management experience in the workforce. I settled, and so can you; I was thousands of dollars in debt, but mine was done through trial and error, and this is why I am sharing my strategy and giving you the necessary tools to fight back, simply by reading this book, which is your individual toolbox for debt settlement. Yes, I have proven principles, and they have worked and will continue to work for you if you use them by the way I have taught you to use them.

Some other debt eliminators are to consolidate bills, like we talked about, before some of the dangers of consolidation. However, if you do have decent credit, this can be an option for those that have not fallen victims to the creditors. Those of you who are considering this option, as I have said before, "tread into this with caution." Bill consolidation can backfire if you are not careful in its usage. In fact, it can end up hurting you just as quickly as it bailed you out in the first place. So this is how it works and how you can maximize its use. The process is a simple one, and using these methods will consolidate high-interest credit cards onto lower-interest credit cards with the lowest interest rates. These savings do happen immediately, but remember the debt is still there, and in the long run, you can end up paying more if the lowest-interest card was a promotional rate and it goes back in six months to where your other cards were before. In fact, some people have reported paying a *higher* rate when the card went up after a promotional offer. So do your homework.

Some other programs allow people who use personal-signature loans to consolidate debts. Again, make sure the rates are lower, and watch what collateral the creditor requires you to put down on the loan. Some people have put homes or cars down as collateral, and then, if they defaulted, they lost their house or car—or both their house *and* car.

So read the fine print if you are using a loan to consolidate debts. In my opinion, if the debt consolidation is unsuccessful, you will end up with "debt accumulation." Watch everything you are doing when taking matters such as these into your own credit hands. I do recommend consulting with a financial planner that has a proven track record in dealing with debt crisis. This is why I continue to be an advocate for settling and/or paying off debt before it becomes delinquent. Always settle after debt becomes delinquent, because the delinquency has already hurt your credit score. Also, use these rules: if you cannot afford it, don't buy it; never charge it—plastic is a quick fix and never the solution. Save up and then purchase when you can pay cash for it.

CHAPTER 3

Debt Reorganization

So let's talk about reorganizing your debt. We have discussed in the previous chapters steps toward setting a budget. Always take into consideration that your own budget is individually designed for you and your family exclusively. Once you have achieved making your budget, you have set the most important financial goal for your future. Now you are heading in the right direction of getting yourself out of debt. Again, do not forget that if you follow these designed principles from this book, you will succeed. These are proven skills; I used them, and they work. While using them, you will also be tracking down where your hard-earned bucks are being spent. This will be one of your biggest allies in maintaining a debt-free lifestyle. By doing so you will be fully in control and not owned by the corporate-giant creditors, collectors, banks, and other financial conglomerates. Never forget who *one* of those enormous giants is, and that is the loan companies. Being in financial self-control is a sure way to keep the financial giants out of your wallets, purses, checking and savings accounts, and financial portfolio. You are now in control of your future financial destiny, and it is vital not to relapse back into the stockpile of financial disaster. I call falling back into financial-misery debt relapsing, because it can be just as devastating as having a drug or alcohol addiction. A debt relapse can crush you and your family in the blink of an eye. Many divorces past and present have been the result of debt relapsing and families having more money going out of the household than earned and falling back into the pit of debt by again running up credit cards and taking out loans to cover their monthly expenses just to survive. When this happens, and a loved one's job is lost due to poor economic times or unemployment, then a lot of families can fall apart at the seams over this financial crisis. I call this a financial head-on collision, and you will truly be buried alive in debt when this relapse occurs. So watch this, and just do not head in that negative direction.

So, we can conclude that:

- Lifestyle change is a key principle and component of debt reorganization.
- Eating in and not out will save you around an extra 25 percent of your income every payday and month.
- This in turn will increase your monthly savings to assist with paying and settling past delinquent debt.
- Savings monthly equals "budget boosters" that help pay off cash advances or delinquent debt.
- If you are getting married or *are* married, putting finances together will also increase your ability to pay off debt faster. "Two is better than one" definitely applies to debt recovery.
- Pay off the highest-interest-rate loans or credit cards with your budget-booster savings.
- Put your spouse on your health-insurance plan. One plan usually saves you money every single month and a lot of insurances give you some break for having family plans versus two individual plans with high premiums.
- Clip coupons, buy generic products (store-brand products), and use reward-card savings at stores that offer rewards.
- My wife and I saved up to $2,000 per month just simply by paying off all cash advances, merging my wife with my healthcare plan, and clipping coupons. We saved like this, and this is how we got ourselves out of debt. We did it together—and so can *you*, folks.
- Apply yourself and make a commitment to yourselves to follow your budget and use the savings to pay off debt—not waste it on adult and children play toys.
- Don't say you can't when you can, and keep paying off that debt in your reorganization phase.

The main thing or objective here is to achieve a debt-free lifestyle. I have listed a lot of items below to make you aware of ways I reorganized debt by not purchasing these listed items.

- Morning coffee—buying it out at a restaurant or coffee house.
- Eating out all three meals.
- Buying excessive amounts of junk food.
- Taking on new loans or debt without paying off existing debt.
- Overextending yourself financially.
- Going on expensive vacations without saving for them and continuing to run your credit-card debt off the chart and maxing your cards out.
- Using credit cards for daily purchases: groceries, clothing, jewelry, and extra items.
- Buying items at full price and not at sale or discounted prices.
- Not conscientiously tracking down your hard-earned bucks.
- Buying luxury items that are nonessential to everyday survival. Especially if you are struggling financially, this is disastrous.

These are only a few listed, but if you follow these tips, it will surely be of great assistance. This is a guide for you to start your own list and track down your bucks. Now that you are on your way to reorganizing your debt, start here and develop your own list, and watch the savings pour back into your monthly budget today. Money is like salt: a pinch here and there goes a long way. It does take time to save money and pay off debt; no doubt there. So at first, just tracking down and saving a few dollars will build up your confidence, and you will start to cruise. Dollars will accumulate in your budget with time and patience. However, the old saying, "actions are bigger than words" applies with reorganizing your personal debt. Presently in these poor economic times, you have to save, as employers are not going to give out raises right now. We are living in an employers' market, so take a load off of your feet by becoming debt free. This is a for-sure raise and one that will keep on giving with time. When I paid off my bills, the next day I started seeing the results, and, needless to say, I was extremely less stressed and more refreshed.

CHAPTER 4

Getting a Jump on Your Credit Score

Getting a jump on your credit score is very important. This is maybe one of the most important decisions you will ever have to make in your life. This, in the long run, will make it possible for you to regain your financial freedom. Even if you have good credit right now, you can still utilize these principles that will assist you in prospering financially and improving your credit score. One of the first things to do in this process is to go online; some companies allow you to purchase a copy of your credit history and credit score for as low as a dollar, whereas others may charge you up to $7.95. This is called an "individual credit report." If you have recently applied for credit, you can receive a free copy through a written request; either way, it's important to get a copy of your credit report. A copy of the credit report will provide you with the information that they have on file of you, and you can see and review what they have been inputting on your individual credit history. Also, you will be able to get the telephone numbers of the creditors where your delinquent accounts are coming from. This way, you will have the ability to contact them and discuss a future potential settlement with them. If you are not getting enough information, use a search engine on your home computer (or, for free, you can go to the public library and use their computers) to search further. If you search for the company by its name, usually you can be successful in locating at least the company's corporate office or business address and telephone number. Next in this process, after locating the company, write a dispute letter to the credit bureau and always put your social security number and delinquent account number with the creditor in your dispute letter. I recommend that a person always ask for the account to be deleted from their credit report and/or listed as paid in full. Be advised here that a lot of companies will list it on your credit report as settled for less then the amount paid. This is not a bad thing, as it is no longer continuing to drag down your credit score, but it does have some impact on your overall score for a period of time.

Remember, if you do not pay the account off first by settlement, there is no point in writing a dispute letter to the credit bureau, as they will not make changes until the account is paid or settled and you can furnish them with the letter from the creditor or collection agency showing that it has been settled or paid off.

Some creditors and collectors will take as low as twenty cents per each dollar owed, like we discussed before. So go ahead when you have the money and negotiate out these delinquent accounts and get rid of them. This is the process of debt elimination. Like I have said before, never pay the collection agency or creditor without getting a settlement letter indicating that they have accepted your settlement offer for the agreed-upon amount between you and them. I did this one time and got totally burned by the collection agency. So after that, I always demanded a settlement-letter acceptance prior to the actual settlement payment itself. The company will usually send this to you by a fax or e-mail; and that is fine, just get one always, with no exceptions. The reputable collection agencies that only want your money will never argue about the letter; if they do argue about it, do not pay them until they comply with your request. *You* are in charge always, not the collector. A good rule here to keep in mind is that if you have not paid on an account for a long period of time, the better you will be able to settle the account for a much lower amount.

Rome was not built in a day; debt elimination is a long process that can take months to resolve, but is well worth your time in the end. Keep this in mind that once you build your credit back, that dream house or car that you have wanted will be at your fingertips, and you will be able to afford them because you will have budgeted and paid off all your delinquent debt. A person that has better credit will also get lower payments and interest rates when purchasing that home or car.

Once you are debt free, you will be among the top 1 percent of the population that can afford to be able to stay in their home without facing foreclosure. I call this the "gold concept," meaning "he/she who has obtained the gold is in charge." So be that golden ruler and strive to have that excellent credit (or at least the best credit that you can get for yourself). This will give you back your buying power and also put a lot more bucks back into your bank account every single month and throughout the year. The difference here is this: when I had poor credit, I was still able to buy a car. Believe me, creditors love high-interest loans to people with poor credit. I ended up paying almost $500 per month (payment was $492.50), and this was for sixty months. It came out to me paying, in the end, $35,000 for a $21,000 car. Wow! I paid almost double for this car by having to go full term. So having poor credit does not pay at all.

I also know now, since I am experiencing a good-credit lifestyle, that with just some pure effort and hard work, you can get rid of that bad credit and buy the car with a much lower interest rate and for a shorter period of time. I usually preach to people to always make a higher monthly payment than asked, and this will make your interest even lower than the actual loan itself. It really is an easy process when you implement it.

So let's talk about some other ways and methods of increasing your credit score. Here are some ideas for credit improvement:

- If your spouse has a better credit score, have him or her add you to their credit card as a user. You will, with time, take on their good credit-reporting rating. I call this "piggy backing" your family's credit.
- Make payments to creditors *always on time*—100 percent of the time.
- Consider seeking assistance from a professional financial adviser. This can be money well spent in the end.
- Do not wait on settling and paying accounts off; do it now.

- Buy a used car instead of a new one, that you can pay cash for without even taking out a loan.

Just sitting around and dehydrating and slowly fading away are not the answer to improving your credit score. If you follow my advice that has been proven time and again, you will be on your way to healthy financial living.

CHAPTER 5

Fighting Back against Debt Collectors

Okay, let me guess: you fell behind on your payments, lost your job, had an emergency bill, illness hit, your child had some unexpected expenses, or, plain and simple, you are buried alive in debt. You could not keep up making the payments on your account or accounts? Did I guess right? Of course I did, and you know it. Yes, unfortunately in the economic system today, this is a very sad reality. Millions of people like yourself are facing foreclosure on their homes or have already been foreclosed on and have lost basically their safe havens. Creditors are getting richer, and the poor are getting even poorer. People nationwide are joining the homeless everyday, and that population is getting younger and younger. This why I have written this book to help those in need fight back and rise up against creditors and these financial institutions and regain their losses.

According to the United States Bureau of Labor Statistics, U.S. Department of Labor, "some 13 million people are out of work, and the unemployment rate is teeter-tottering from 9.2 to 8.6 percent (April–October). November of 2011 had the highest unemployment with some slight improvement to 8.6 percent." If you ask me "why this is the trend?" I will tell you the creditors and collection agencies are pounding all of us into the ground, turning us into financial oblivion just like granules of sand.

So, the next question is, what do we as consumers do to fight back? As consumers, we need to exercise our rights under the Fair Debt Collection Practices, Act 15 USC 1692g Sec. 809B. This way, you can confirm and make sure that the debt is actually yours. Make the creditor tell you exactly what account is yours, how much you owe, and never agree to pay on a debt until the creditor has furnished you with all the requested information. Believe me, you know, and when you see what they have provided, you will know if it's legitimate. As much as a lot of us may want to play it off or down, we know what we have out there as debt. I knew when I had a $10,000, $5,000, or even a $2,500 loan—and you know, too. Let's be honest with ourselves and take responsibility for that. We signed the papers, so we are not going to be in financial denial either. We need to be honest and not ignore the problem any more. I am not going to guide you toward any method of defrauding anyone, not even a collection agency. Fraud is illegal, and we taxpayers end up paying for that, too. So being honest and real is the only solution. Please, everyone, do not forget this rule: "Honesty is always the best policy." I will teach you methods and ways to settle these debts, but let's agree to take responsibility for our actions for the debt we did create. No one twisted our arms to take those loans or credit cards. Debt settlement is honest and is the quickest way to deal with the debt collector and collection agency. Avoiding phone calls, waiting for statute of limitations to get rid of the credit problems are not the solutions to your problems. This is like being an ostrich and putting your head in the sand. I will warn you that some collection agencies and creditors are not selling wolf tickets when they say they will get a judgment against you. Some of these agencies actually do have attorneys, and they can take legal action against you. This is why debt settlement, even in it's early stages, is still your best option and will avoid any legal ramification against you in the future.

In my opinion, debt settlement is the best way to deal with delinquent debt. Here are some ways to fight back against a creditor/collector:

- Check and make sure the collection agency is a legitimate company
- Make them send you all documentation showing you owe them.
- Do not give out any personal information to a collector when conversing with him or her.

- Never give them a personal address where they could serve you with legal papers, usually a legal-judgment process.
- Call the collector, but only call them when you have enough funds to negotiate and settle out the debt. Remember, they will keep your telephone number on file when you call them.
- Be a hard negotiator, but realize the collector and his agency do have minimal amounts that they can accept in the end.
- Try not to make them your enemy. Instead try to get them to sympathize with your problem.
- Do not let your guard down with sweet-talking collectors; their job is to get your money.
- Never pay the full amount of a delinquent debt. Always negotiate a much lower amount. It is already delinquent and has hurt your credit report so why pay more when you can save money and pay less with the same results.
- Always get a final payoff letter from the creditor or collector you settled the debt with a send a copy, not the original, to the credit bureau. Keep your original in a file forever.
- The final rule here is to take responsibility. Do not listen to other people's advice on how they beat the system by using statute of limitations on delinquent accounts. This is foolish and may even get you sued in the end. People that give out advice like this are using Ponzi schemes and are usually committing fraud themselves. These people are better known as white-collar criminals. On the flip side, they may even be one of those people leeching and living off of Mom or Dad.
- Most collection agencies and collectors will want to negotiate with you, so this is a process that works for everyone involved.
- The quicker you settle the debt, the quicker you can move on with your life. "Actions are bigger than words, and get rid of debt."

CHAPTER 6

Fighting Our Banks on Mortgages

Today, approximately three million people have lost their homes due to foreclosures (as we just talked about in chapter 5) that are in turn due to a recession and people losing their jobs. People have just given up on their fight against creditors and, in some cases, have rolled over and given up entirely. Do not do this, as you have some ammunition in dealing with the banks on mortgages. If you are in the process of losing your home, there are seminars out there that can assist you in loan-modification programs and other programs for those in mortgage problems. These seminars and special conferences will go over and review with you your original loan documents and let you know what options they recommend and what you have available in your current situation. A lot of people have found solutions to their mortgage complications simply by attending and following the expert's advice. These special programs are sometimes even funded by the federal government and are there to assist you, but if you do not take advantage or research these programs then they cannot and will not help you if you do not attend them or follow the advice they provide. Many of these programs have been implemented due to fraud and mortgage companies taking advantage of us consumers. This why today the federal government has cracked down on unscrupulous prime-loan lenders that were legally ripping off us consumers and putting a lot of us into loans that we should never have been allowed to qualify for in the first place and then forcing us into foreclosure.

This is definitely some information that mortgage lenders do not want you as a consumer to know. Did you know that lenders will even pay you to leave your house if they foreclose on you? Yes, in many cases, lenders have done just that.

Lenders have even paid homeless squatters that move into a vacant, foreclosed home to leave the premises. And it's not hundreds of dollars, either; it's in the *thousands*—on average, around $5,000 to $7,000 just to vacate the empty home that they illegally moved into in the first place. Ridiculous, yes, but very real, as they just want to get the property sold and in some other consumer's hands to bleed them financially. Lenders are all about making the big bucks, and they spend money to make lots more money. I personally heard of a homeless man on the central coast in California that got $7,500 by one of the largest mortgage lenders in the nation to leave a home he was illegally squatting in. Wow! Imagine that scenario, if all the homeless knew about those meal tickets. These rich lenders and banks do not want all of us to know these things, and they want to keep us in the dark and oblivious to what they do behind the scenes. Yes, having knowledge is powerful, and rich-bank corporate America only wants to keep ripping us little-people consumers off.

So guess what? Now is the time for all of us consumers to fight back in this financial revolution. I am glad to say that I will be the first consumer to lead the fight for all the little people in the world, because this is a fight we must not back down from, or the rich will keep kicking all of us down and getting richer while we get poorer and end up destitute. The rich will continue to have million-dollar yachts and play polo and have dinner parties. In the meantime, *we* are all starving to death and cannot afford to put gas in our cars to do anything and barely even get to work—that is how pathetic our economic system has become.

Another myth stating "you can never pay your mortgage late" is only a myth—because you can. I myself once got strapped for money, and even though the lender can charge you the consumer a late fee, the lender cannot foreclose as long as you never miss two payments in a row. Paying late is not a foreclosable offense, and you can keep and remain in your home as a late payer. Do not forget the fees will accumulate, but the way I look at it, on a thirty-year loan, who really cares? I ended up selling the home long before I ever caught up on the late payment fees, and I made money on the sale and wiped out the loan when I sold the house. I lived in that home for over five years, and the old adage here is "as long as you pay, you can stay." It does save you money to pay on time, but there is no prison for late payers.

Today, we the people are just trying to survive and maintain having the basic fundamentals of life. We consumers are not getting $375,000 in speaker's fees; we are making minimum wage and trying to put food on the table and have clothing and shelter for ourselves and family members. Again, we are the poor people who struggle because we work and pay our taxes without loopholes or paying off lobbyists in Washington DC with our own hidden agendas like the rich do every day.

Let me give you all some advice. If you are in a high-interest home loan and have the ability to get into a thirty-year, lower-interest, fixed-rate home loan, then do it right now. Your payments will be a lot lower and very affordable. This way, you will be able to make your home-mortgage payments on time. The new payment will be budget friendly and work for you and your family. Yes, "positive results bring positive effects." Hope is on the way, and you are now heading in the right direction. You are in charge of your own financial, home-loan freedom and destiny in this financial revolution. Where people really get in trouble is when they panic on their home and feel that a short sale is their only option. This is a ludicrous attitude. So, keep paying your payments and remember the stock principle "keep when low and sell when they reach their peak." Real estate and homes always bounce back with time, and the market changes, as we all know, daily and yearly. So keep the property and wait it out so you can sell it when the market rebounds. In the meantime, it is still better to own your own home than be a renter and not have any equity or anything to show for with your payments. Never do a short sale; that will look almost as bad on your credit as a foreclosure. I myself would rather be foreclosed on and make the lender pay me to move, as they have been doing to squatters. Anyway, if you have a home, keep it in this bad selling time, and wait for the market to rebound; do not give it away on a short sale as only the banks and lenders gain from that. During the short sale, you the consumer are living in the home, maintaining it for the bank, and then, in the end, they sell it out from underneath you, and your credit is ruined in the process. So bad odds; do not agree to those terms.

CHAPTER 7

Why Now Is the Time to Buy a Home and Not Rent

Presently, with the increase in the unemployment rate, short sales, and foreclosures, the consumer renter is paying a stiff price. Landlords know that they can charge higher rents because people are so desperate for housing options, especially those who have recently suffered losing their homes. A lot of these landlords have become financial opportunists. This also has given a lot of them the ability to legally become slumlords and not take care of properties but continue to increase rents and demands on their tenants. Some of housing these slumlords are managing are barely livable structures, are run down, are in poor areas, and are in need of major repairs that the slumlords never intend to have done.

Because of slumlords, this in itself should encourage those who are able to qualify for a home loan to get motivated, get off the couch, and start house hunting. In fact, many lenders currently are offering lower-interest-rate loans to first-time homebuyers. There are numerous programs out there for everyone, from USDA loans to FHA, HUD, VA, and a lot of other programs to suit your individual needs. Again, by improving your credit, you will be able to make a purchase through one of these programs. Yes, with improved credit and a higher credit score, you and your family will be able to fit a new mortgage payment right into your budget, because it will be lower and at a lower interest rate. Now, instead of making your landlord rich by paying out high rent money to him and paying the mortgage *for* him on *his* rental property, you will be building up your own equity in your own house, and, in a lot of cases, your mortgage will be lower than renting in this buyer's market. Plus, you will be able to make your property your family's dream house and put your own individual stamp on the home, making improvements that you want in order to make it more enjoyable to live in.

No worries on putting some upgrades in your home, because when you do decide to sell to get a different home, that is where a lot of your hard work will come back to you in your own pocket. A lot of times, for example, a $20,000 upgrade that you do can later increase the home's value by another *$40,000*, so you have increased your equity by $20,000. The rule here is that the longer you stay in the home, in most cases, the more equity you will accumulate over time. With a lot of homes, after five years of ownership, a seller can get double the amount they paid for the home, with improvements and upgrades along the way. So, with real estate ownership, you can make money while you are living inside the house.

My wife and I are still searching the Internet and meeting with our real estate broker and house hunting. I am also waiting to finalize the approval of my Veterans Home Loan. A few years ago, with my poor credit, this would not even have been a dream, but today it is a reality with improved and good credit. We have probably looked at, on the Internet and in person, well over sixty homes so far, and we will continue to look until we find that home that meets our needs, is the best house at the best price, has the lowest possible payment for that type of property, and of course the largest lot and backyard for that lowest price. I have owned, on my own, a fixer-upper before, and it was a huge project, so this time we are looking for a home that can have some small projects but is at least able to be moved into right away with minimal improvements needed. Here are some helpful home-buying tips that have helped us along the way and will save you time and money if you follow them:

Home-Buying Tips

- When qualifying for a loan, find a reputable lender that best suits your financial needs
- Make sure you have followed the principles of this book in cleaning up your individual credit scores.

Remember: the better your credit score, the lower the interest rate will be on the loan.

- Find a real estate agent who is reputable and whom you like, because you will be spending a lot of time with him or her. I recommend getting a prequalification letter prior to even looking at homes. You cannot buy the home if you cannot qualify for the loan in the first place, so get a prequalification letter ahead of time from your lender.
- Ask your real estate agent to carefully screen properties for back taxes and liens and to get a property history.
- When you do get approved for the loan, I recommend getting a thirty-year, fixed-rate mortgage, especially if you plan on living in the house long-term. The fixed-rate mortgage, in my opinion, is the safest and has good interest rates with a good credit score. Do not forget that everyday interest rates change, so always take that into consideration when dealing with your loan.
- Always try and purchase your dream home when the interest rates are down and it's a buyers market. Presently, you are in good shape, as interest rates currently are at all-time lows in the current market, and home prices are down.
- So if you do not get a home while the going is good, it may be much more expensive and harder at a later time. The rule to buy when it's low and sell when it's high is extremely applicable right now. So do not wait if you are able to make that purchase.
- If possible, use a direct lender for your loan and that in itself could save you thousands of dollars in fees on your home loan.
- The Internet is a great way to find direct lenders for the loans you are seeking out.
- Beware that there are a lot of money pits out there, so really have your agent give you all the details on the

home and always ask for a home inspection prior to going into escrow.

- Never, ever, buy a home that is out of your monthly budget price range. Do not let any real estate agent talk you into a more expensive home just because you qualify for more on your home loan. Ultimately, *you* have to pay the monthly mortgage payment, not your agent. In fact, agents get between 3 to 7 percent on the sale of a home. So naturally they want you to buy a more expensive home, because they get a higher commission.
- Do not focus on refrigerators and appliances in the home or the home lacking them. You can always buy a washing machine or refrigerator on sale, or even used, at very reasonable prices. These you can use when you first move in or until you can afford better ones at a later time.
- Form a check-off list on what you want and desire out of your new dream home. Do not buy the home until the boxes have been checked off that meet your needs and demands.
- Do not forget that once you sign the papers and escrow is completed, you are the homeowner, and at that point, it is a done deal. So if the home has problems, they now become yours exclusively.
- Go for it and start house hunting now—do not wait.

Personally, I believe the benefits of home ownership outweigh being a renter by far. Owning your own home in this market not only will be a good investment in the next five years, but it will save you money every single month, and at the end of the year, you will get money back for owning your own home. This is very tax efficient, and your home is not only your dream, but also an equity builder; and that is where the sky is the limit on how much you can prosper in years to come.

CHAPTER 8

Refinancing If You Own Your Home

If you have been making payments on time and have not been late more than one time on your mortgage payment, there are federal programs available to you out there. All you have to do is investigate them and find one for you. I would personally recommend finding one to take advantage of and refinancing your home as soon as possible. Here are some reasons that will assist you in making your decision to refinance.

Reasons to Refinance

- Refinancing will help you and your family keep from losing your home to the bank, especially if your mortgage has skyrocketed and is too high.
- A refinance with a much lower interest rate could save you hundreds of dollars every month. This in turn will make your house payment more budget driven and less stressful and burdensome for you and your family. It will take a financial load right off your shoulders.
- Presently mortgage refinance rates are at their lowest. So here is your reward for making your house payments on time, and now you will get a much lower interest rate and monthly payment.
- Congratulations! Now your home ownership is more enjoyable because it's more affordable.
- A refinance can save your home from falling into foreclosure, because you will be able to make the payment.

- It just makes sense to refinance and pay less in the long run.
- When you refinance, you can even pick a different lender if your old lender was hard to deal with, was hard to get ahold of, or was not responsive to your needs.
- Refinancing puts more money back into your budget and savings account every single month, saving thousands yearly.

These reasons listed above are only a small drop in the bucket as to why you should refinance. But keep in mind that if you are going to save hundreds of dollars per month, then just go for it and don't look back.

A huge way you can save money in a refinance is if you are a veteran of the United States military. Now listen to me carefully, veterans: if you have bought your home without using your VA Home Loan, now is the time to qualify for that VA Home Loan. Does a VA streamline refinance? These VA loans have the best interest rates and virtually cannot be beat. A lot fees are paid during this process, and there are a lot of savings by using the VA streamline. Your mortgage specialist will go over all the details, and believe me, you will be very happily surprised at your monthly savings compared to what you are paying now. You deserve a financial break for your service to your country, and there is no higher honor, so let your hard work for once take a financial burden off of you and your family.

A lot of veterans ask if it's too hard to qualify. Heck no, it's easy! You can go online and print off from the Veterans Administration homepage an application for a Certificate of Eligibility for the VA Home Loan. It takes a whole five to ten minutes to fill out. The VA usually gets you approved in thirty to sixty days or sooner, depending on how you can show proof of your military-service time by a DD214 form. If you do not have your DD214, then write to the records department in Saint Louis, Missouri. The VA has all the information on their Web site. Once you get your COE (Certificate of Eligibility), give your lender a copy of it, and you have now qualified for the VA loan from the VA. Now, if you have at least a 620 or above credit score, most lenders will qualify you for your VA loan. Some lenders do want to see a 640–660 credit score, and, of course, all lenders will need to see that you have proof of employment or permanent disability benefits. You must meet the criteria for approved credit score in order to qualify.

If you are not a military veteran then there are a lot of other programs out there that are available. For instance, some areas have area-specific government home loans such as USDA, FHA, HUD, and the new Obama home-loan plan. Wait—there is more, especially for the first-time homebuyer or those who are refinancing. Like I recommended before, if at all possible always try to use a direct lender on whatever loan plan you are choosing, to take advantage of not only the lower rates but also the reduction in fees from using a direct lender. Also pick only the loan that benefits you the most, and never let any mortgage specialist talk you into a loan that does not benefit you the most or has a higher mortgage payment than you can afford. You are the only one that ultimately has to live with whatever decision you make in the end. Do not forget there are fees associated with refinancing. So when the time comes, and if you sell or take the loan to full term, it will chip away at your home's equity. The golden rule for refinancing your home purchasing is when the mortgage rates drop, then refinance or purchase. Buy when it's low, and sell when your property reaches its peak high. Remember, currently in this market, it's cheaper in a lot of instances to buy than rent.

In my opinion, direct lenders are better to do your loans with because they can really save you a bundle of money on your loan. Why? Because the middleman regular-mortgage-company mom-and-pop shop charge you exorbitant fees, and this is how they stay in business. A direct lender, on the other hand, is counting more on doing large quantities of loans due to lower rates, and so the more loans they do, the more they make. Mom-and-pop mortgage-company shops try to gouge, once you apply, with high loan fees. Also, the small companies need to be watched for reputability and much higher mortgage payments when the loan is finalized. These smooth-talking loan specialists in these shops like to hide fees in the context of your loan documents. So beware if you chose one of these companies.

So again, when taking out any loan, investigate the loan type, inquire about fees, and never take anything for face value that a mortgage specialist/ broker ever tells you. Before signing any loan, make sure that it is the best possibly designed loan for your and your family's budget. Never let anyone pressure you into a loan. Take your time when picking a mortgage company, and look at customer reviews and feedback. Compare their mortgage rates with other companies' rates. Search on the Internet for direct lenders, and see how their rates compare with your companies' rates. Just keep in mind, like we have said before, that interest rates change daily. I have listed some warning signs below to assist you with your loan.

Loan Warning Signs

- Watch for fine-print tactics to not openly disclose some additional hidden fees.
- Mortgage brokers charging extra points against your loan, which gives them more money on your loan.
- Lender also hiding fees.
- Being talked into a loan that has high interest rates and mortgage payments that you cannot afford. If you cannot afford the home, then do not buy it.
- Being talked into a short-term, five- to seven-year ARM loan instead of a safe, thirty-year, fixed-rate loan.
- ARM loans will backfire on you at the end of term, and you may end up losing your home if you do not qualify to refinance your loan.
- Get the lowest rate; do not sign up for a much higher rate, which means higher payment.

These are only a few—but critical—warning signs. Do your homework and research when applying for a loan. Be your own loan detective and investigate thoroughly all aspects of the loan before signing the loan documents. Once you sign the loan papers, the house and loan become your problem. So always remember: let the buyer beware, and make sure that when you sign the line, you have total peace of mind and true ownership excitement.

CHAPTER 9

Settling Debt

This chapter will be going into detail about how you can settle debt. There are some strategies, and, like I have said in earlier chapters, it does take time to completely settle the debt. Since you have your toolbox (your book) right here, this process will be a whole lot easier than it was for myself. Hopefully, it will be less time consuming for you. This I am happy to provide, because it took me an enormous amount of time to figure all of this out. So simply by reading this book and applying these provided principles, you will be way ahead of the debt-settlement game and be successful in finalizing your debt settlement. See some of the strategies below.

Debt-Settlement Strategies

- Make an inventory of all your debts and list them on a piece of paper.
- Number each account starting with the number one, and list them straight down the piece of paper.
- Off to the side of each account write down the amount you owe on that account.
- Calculate total amount owed of all accounts.
- Then figure out what 20 to 25 percent of each account is and write that beside each account.
- Propose an offer starting with the first creditor/collector on your list, based upon that 20–25 percent figure.

I personally had ten accounts, which came out to a grand total of approximately $47,500. The reason I used "approximately" is because before I started my strategy, I had a few offers already in the working and had paid off several others. So it was actually way worse than my $47,500 figure. However, by using my own proven strategy, I settled all of these ten accounts for a total of $11,500. Remember, your totals will be different; this is just what mine came out to. This is just a rough guide as to what you will be capable of doing after reading and following these tips, principles, and strategies. I saved $36,000 by settling my own debt. (See, when you thought there was no hope, it was right around the corner and at your disposal.) Still, it took me some time, and it does require patience. I had to wait a lot of the time to save up so I did have enough money to be able to make a settlement offer. I guarantee you it will happen, and that can be very frustrating, but in the end, to be debt free was a huge relief. It is also hard to stop paying those ridiculous monthly payments that get you nowhere, because everyone is afraid to do it. I will admit I was, and then, when I started saving the money I was paying out, I realized that I was definitely on the right path and letting them fall into delinquency. If they are not delinquent the collector/creditor will not agree to a settlement offer. So why pay? Just let them fall into delinquency so you can settle them immediately when you have the money. You will not go to jail, as there is no debtors' prison; remember that saying.

However, if you *are* tracked down, which rarely occurs, and served with a judgment, then it's time to borrow money from a family member or good friend or make whatever offers you can get them to accept. This does not usually occur, but keep that in mind always when dealing with collectors and creditors. The name of the game is to settle the debt before it ever goes that far anyway.

Some collection agencies and debt collectors will agree on extremely high-balance accounts to let you make zero interest payments on them monthly. This is a good deal for you and them. I did do this on three of my accounts, and when I got them down to where I could afford to settle them, I made an offer, and because the collector had received steady payments, they accepted my low settlement offers. So this does work, especially if you owe over $5,000 on any given account, as it takes time to pay them down, but with no interest, your payment goes right off the entire balance and takes that high balance down, over time, fairly fast.

I did do this on an $8,000 account that was a personal-signature loan with a collection agency, and after fifteen monthly payments with zero interest, they settled the account for around $3000. So making payments is an option, but I have found that when you do not make payments, the collector takes less in a settlement offer. When you are making payments, the collector knows that you have a job and money, so they want a piece of your earnings. When you do not pay, they do not know if you have a job or money, so they are worried that you may disappear, and they will never get paid; and that is where the 25 percent settlement on the dollar really starts to be accepted by them. I do have one rule, as I detailed earlier, and that is I never settle for more than sixty cents on the dollar.

I learned very quickly that when I had saved money and was making a lump-sum settlement offer, the collector would take less. So I always waited them out until they came down to at least fifty to fifty-five cents on the dollar (or way less: at twenty to twenty-five cents, is the best, of course). Do watch out, because collectors will access your credit report, and they are trained to find out what you gain by settling the account. Several collectors I was dealing with saw that I had applied to a few mortgage companies for a home loan. So right away they knew I needed to get the account off my credit report to be able to qualify. I did play it off and told them I got denied because I did not have enough money, and they bought it. Do be careful, though, as you can see what can happen. Collection agencies will keep track of any telephone number you call them from, so keep that in mind, and if you are making payments to them, use a PO box, never your home address. Collectors do use a lot of financial detective work, so you have to be on top of your game, thinking one step ahead of them. This will keep the collector guessing and get them to fall for a low debt-settlement offer.

Remember what you have been taught about how collectors will lie to you when settling debt; so what I am advocating is turning the tables on them. I never advocate someone to lie, just to settle for what you can pay and afford, not the amount the collector is originally asking. Always negotiate to save yourself money. Collectors make huge profits on delinquent accounts, so there is plenty of room to settle them for way less than the asking amount. This where we are dealing with a financial revolution, so fight back against these huge agencies with low offers and settlements, and take charge of your life and credit once and for all.

I have spoken to many creditors and, unfortunately, numerous collection agencies when I was settling my own debt from suffering from a bad divorce, and simply passing on my problem to the collectors and collection agencies did buy me a lot of mileage in getting the accounts settled. Just about anyone knows that divorces happen all the time and even collectors have a hard time not bending the rules a little bit to help you out. Be a professional salesman: make an offer and then take it away when and if they counteroffer you too high. Also let them know you have other financial obligations with other creditors and that if they don't take your offer, someone else will, and you may not be able to pay them for a year or two. They will buckle under that kind of pressure, and the collector will worry that if they don't take the offer, they could be left out in the cold with you not paying them. Being confident, firm, and standing your ground when negotiating a settlement offer is of vital importance in lowballing a creditor/collector.

Other Strategies in Settling Debt

- After you agree with the creditor/collector on a settlement offer, then finalize the deal.
- Make sure you get a settlement letter from the creditor/collector stating the agreed-upon settlement amount before paying them.
- Ask for the letter to be sent by fax or e-mail to speed up the process.
- Once you get the letter, which is your proof that they have agreed to the lower settlement amount, then pay

them by using an ACH electronic payment and having it post on your payday or whatever day is convenient for you. Most collectors ask for no more than two weeks of post-dating the ACH transaction, which they will automatically deduct from your checking account on the date you agree for it to process.

- Once paid, after thirty days, ask for a payoff letter.
- When you receive the payoff letter, send one copy (never the original, which you keep and file) to the three credit bureaus: Experian, Equifax, and Trans Union. Once this is complete, you will usually have to wait thirty to forty-five days for them to update your request in changing the status of the delinquent account to paid and or settled.

The key to debt settlement is patience and perseverance. It will not be an easy process, but again, by using the tools you have learned from this book, you are armed with financial ammunition. You will win the debt battle and will be able to do it fairly expeditiously with the tools you have, just as long as you use them correctly. I have spent hours of long, hard research and late nights studying these tools—and they work. They worked for me, and if that was the case, they will surely work for you. My mission is to help people like you, who are buried in debt, find the solution to get out of debt. Your life will already be taking a turn for the better if you follow my guidelines. You will have a better quality of life with your debt-stress-free lifestyle and a great credit score empowering your future as a home-buying consumer—or just peace of mind being debt free.

CHAPTER 10

The Final Act of Empowerment

I spent years working as a professional counselor in the field of substance-abuse counseling. I truly believe that an addiction, if it goes unnoticed and untreated, will completely destroy the individual and can and will even result in death. Right now, people, we have another addiction out there, and it is not a drug—it is bad-debt addiction. This addiction is consuming people and destroying families. Many people struggle with this horrific addiction every single day of their life. Yes, there was period when I was you, and I was that person. I went through a bad divorce, but I will make no excuses; I allowed myself to fall into this addiction—and so did you. I was there, but today I am *not* there, because I decided to stop the addiction and take action. Of course, I jokingly will say divorcing my ex-wife did help, since she left me to pay for some major debts that she was responsible for. However, many others continue to be denial and live that lifestyle of bad-debt syndrome. To the people that do live that lifestyle running up bills and loans and maxing out credit cards, there does come a day when the creditor says, "No more; it's time to pay up." I call this the day of reckoning, and when a bad-debt addict is forced to get help, then this is where their new beginning happens. I call this the bad-debt awakening process. So when you are here, it does not matter how you got here. What matters is, like with a bad drug, *how are you going to cope and deal with this problem?* Yes, right now is where the getting clean and debt free starts. Here are some self-empowerment tools to assist you in getting clean and debt free and not relapsing back into the bad-debt lifestyle:

Self-Empowerment Tools

- Realize you are the one in debt, and take responsibility for your bad-debt actions. I want you to say, "I will fight this problem."
- Read this book to entirety and use the tools, principles, and tips provided.
- Start an exercise program—walking, swimming, or yoga, for example; really, anything with aerobic activity is always good. Throwing in some weightlifting here and there for muscle toning is a great idea. You choose your activity, but get off of the couch and do something *right now today*.
- Say to yourself, "I know I can conquer this debt and take action. I have knowledge and will conquer the debt, as knowledge is power."
- Seek the help of a financial planner. I have listed one in the last chapter that can help you out if in need.
- Contact the creditor/collector and negotiate a debt settlement of the delinquent accounts.
- Make sure after settling the debt you get a payoff letter from each creditor/collector, and send them to the three credit bureaus I have told you about. Only send copies; you always maintain the original in a file for yourself.
- In my opinion, keep one credit card for emergencies, but pay any charges off by the end of the month and try and maintain a zero balance on the one card.
- Do not take on new debt after you pay off the old; the purpose is to become as debt free as possible.
- Start an individual retirement account. Many financial gurus advise in starting a Roth IRA. In my opinion, I agree with these financial gurus, and I myself have a Roth IRA. I have watched the IRA make me money over time, and it's working.
- Say to yourself, "I am in charge of my life and my finances. I am the keeper of my own debt-and-finance key. I am the only one that either helps or harms me."
- "I will get rid of debt; this is unconditional."

Having a Family Debt Intervention

- Sit all family members in a circle in the living room.
- Remind your spouse and children that now is the time to become budget conscious, and it will be this way from here out.
- Under no circumstances while trying to eliminate debt will we as a family charge on any credit cards or take on new debt.
- If your spouse is irresponsible with credit cards, cut them up and cancel them. Let your spouse know they will not be reopened.
- Tell your irresponsible spouse you have made an appointment with a financial counselor, you will both follow the professional's financial advice, and this is the way it is going to be.
- Discuss with the entire family that junk food is expensive and will be drastically reduced.
- Let each family member know that each person has to help out in order to reduce debt as a family. It's a team effort.
- Take charge of the checkbook and only have one person in charge. The most responsible parent should be in charge. Only have one checkbook with one person monitoring and paying bills. Both parents can discuss and show bill-paying accountability, but have only one checking-account manager.
- Let your spouse know that any purchase over twenty dollars will be discussed together and will not be done unless in agreement with each other as a team.
- Never let children be in charge; a parent always is in control.
- Stick firmly by your family's planned budget.
- Track all bucks spent. Remember: "tracking the bucks saves money."
- Use the emergency credit card only for emergencies—never for vacations or shopping.

- Stop trying to keep up with neighbors or friends. Eliminate the "keeping up with the Joneses" syndrome. You are in charge of your family, so who cares? Only *you* should care. No play toys, motorcycles, boats, RVs, expensive bicycles, and so on until you can afford one and pay cash.
- If you finding yourself starting to debt relapse, immediately make an appointment with your financial advisor and get help immediately; do not wait until the bottom falls out of your checkbook.

Tools for Financial Recovery

- Make yourself accountable for your actions. Never forget, when everything is paid off, the past miserable-debt-self problems.
- Focus on your positive, debt-free future, and utilize your learned principles in your everyday life.
- Do not accumulate new debt.
- Eliminate extra, nonessential items unless they are for daily survivability.
- Cut down on eating out and junk foods, and go out to eat as a family only as a reward for following your budget. Possibly try and restrict eating out to one time every ninety days.
- Sell play toys, boats, RVs, motorcycles, collections, and whatever else can generate you the needed money to pay off the delinquent debt. Having a yard sale is a good way to generate extra money. Out with the old, and pay off debt now.
- When shopping for groceries, use reward cards, clip coupons, and buy sale items instead of non-sale items.
- Budget as a way of life, and commit to that.

Believe me, I know it is not easy to strictly follow a budget. The budget process does work, but it must be followed every day. Commit to following your budget for thirty days, and reward yourself and your family after you have successfully completed that thirty days. Then target another sixty days and continue that process. Do not forget to reward you and your family every time you complete the target dates of your budget. The longer you follow the budget, the easier it does get. Budgeting will become your new lifestyle, and it will become routine, the same as dressing yourself or putting on your shoes every day. We are all creatures of habit, so the process does work. Track your bucks every day so you know where all your money is spent, and keep everyone and yourself accountable at all times for following the strict budget rules.

Setting Financial Goals

We are now in a critical phase in your financial-recovery process. This is establishing goals—where you hope to be in five or ten years (called "long-term financial goals"). But before we go that long term, let's have a one-year long-term goal as our first target. Also, you must have one short-term financial goal for the next thirty days. You see how this works? You have one long-term financial goal and one short-term financial goal. In the long-term goal, you may want ask yourself these questions below:

Long-Term Financial Goals

- What are my future financial dreams?
- Will I buy a house or sell the one I have and downsize?
- What are my financial hopes and desires?

Long-Term Goal Exercise

- Start a journal for the next ninety days.
- Make daily entries for your financial hopes and dreams and desires.

- Have one short-term financial goal included in the journal as well. The short-term goal should target a thirty-day period.
- Review the journal at the end of the thirty-day period, and give yourself a grade of A, B, C, D, or F. Check and see if you have completed those thirty-day short-term goals. Then, after this, target the next sixty days, completing the entire ninety-day period, and give yourself another grade. This will help you measure how your goals are going and how successful you have been in following your individual goals.
- Remember, if you achieved one or two of your goals, then you did great, and that deserves an A grade. If one goal was not achieved, then you must have to focus on weekly and daily short-term goals before targeting back on your long-term goals. This process will help you stay focused.
- Remember, once you complete short-term goals, then the long-term goals can be worked on and achieved.
- If you are very motivated, and over two goals were completed, then move on and keep going; you are steam rolling, and your goals are that much closer to reality. Isn't it great to know they will come true?
- At the end of every six-month period, sit down with a professional financial planner and discuss with the planner your six-month progress.
- Read your journal at the end of the year, and see just how much progress you have made. You will be amazed at how you and your family did for following your one-year plan and for financial-goal completion and progress.

Not only do a lot of financial planners provide great solid financial advice, but they can also assist you with improving and developing better plans and goals to increase your level of goal completion financially.

I will give you some personal insight and success that I went through personally. My wife and I set a goal for me to pay off all of my debt in one year. With a lot of saving and my wife's help, this became a reality. We worked hard, and we actually achieved that long-term goal in eight months. We did so well that we even paid off some debt that Jan had from the past as well. I was able to negotiate debt settlements with every single collector/creditor, averaging between twenty-five cents to fifty-five cents on the dollar. This eliminated thousands of dollars of debt. Yes, we both felt a huge weight come off of our family's shoulders. Being debt free is like no other feeling you can ever imagine. If we did it, so can you; just work at it, and set your goals for your financial future.

Vital Parts of Self-Empowerment

- Keep yourself mentally fit to stay healthy.
- Positive thinking brings positive results financially. You must stay calm but assertive with debt collectors when settling debt.

Financial Positive Thinking

- Believe in yourself and be a pit-bull negotiator always striving to lowball the collector.
- Say to yourself, "Today is a great day, and I will succeed."
- Say to yourself, "My actions will prevail with dealing with and conquering my creditors/collectors."
- I commit to the financial-revolution cause and fight financially the creditors, financial corporate giants, and collection agencies, until they are all lowballed and settled with my individual debt; and at no time will I pay the full amount with their imposed interest rates.
- I will use my taught principles and tools to fight these unscrupulous financial institutions.
- I will work hard, always maintaining my financial success, hopes, and dreams and to become debt free.

- I will commit myself to live a debt-free lifestyle. This way, I am not assisting to keep these financial giants in business by giving them my hard-earned money.
- Debt free means stress free, so I will strive for that type of lifestyle.
- I will defeat debt and those corporations and creditors, and the collection agencies that are funded by them. I will do this by never again utilizing their services.
- Every day I will work hard to not financially relapse back into my past debt ever again.
- I will stay financially healthy one day at a time and not take on more then I can handle for that one day.

So now we have established that attacking debt is a daily process, and it can be a struggle, no doubt. There are going to be hurdles and obstacles along the way to financial freedom. I do recommend to keep yourself mentally healthy, only taking on one account at a time and seeing it all the way through to final settlement before attempting another one. Settling debt can be slow and arduous, so this is not the time to be multitasking; it's the time to be focused. In my opinion, working first on the lower-balance account is the best, because usually at the beginning of the debt-settlement process, you have the least amount of money, because you are still buried in the debt. As time progresses and you have much larger monetary reserves, you can attack those big, major-financial-draining accounts. Plus, every time you settle an account, I guarantee you that you will start to feel better, less stressed, and really start to feel hopeful that you can and will live a debt-free lifestyle. This will be done, of course, in the near future if you follow this book's tools.

Remember when you were a kid and your mother read you the story about the little train that wanted to climb the mountain, and eventually he got his dream? Well, here you go; be that train, and through your hard work, determination, positive thinking, and settling the debt, you will be on your life path to financial freedom. The main thing is not to worry or panic; that will only make things worse, and the problem will still be there. So gear up, and don't let depression conquer you. Take action, exercise, and stay and eat healthy during the debt-conquering process. The more debt you settle, the more positive you will feel, and your level of optimism will skyrocket off the chart.

We may not want to believe this and may accept it or not: bad debt can be passed down from one generation to the next. How does/can this occur? Well, let's explore how this happens.

Bad Debt Passed Down from One Generation to the Next

- A family member becomes sick or dies and leaves his property and valuables to his family members. These properties of course have liens and/or taxes owed on them. The person listed in the will now has to pay off these old taxes and liens before assuming the real property, or the state will take them from them anyways.
- A family member or your own child runs up and maxes out their credit cards and then asks you to help pay them off. This really bites, but it can happen.
- Your mother or aunt taught you that shopping or using credit cards for daily use is an okay thing to do. Learned patterns of behavior are hard to break, especially with credit-card use and abuse.
- Family members justify using credit cards and taking out loans, stating, "The banks own everything anyway, so why not live it up?"
- Your parents die in debt, and so you follow that pattern of behavior.

So, right now is the time to break the cycle of financial addiction. It's the time to become debt free and clean from the dredges of financial addiction. Financial addiction has consumed you for way too long, and it's time to stop the cycle of addiction, being broke and stressed out, and being consumed by debt. These tools and principles you are learning will allow you to be clean and free of bad debt entirely. This is your new way of life, and you have a fresh start. Once you are able to take responsibility and take charge of your personal finances, which includes total and complete debt elimination, then you are back on track. Do not wait, my friends, today is the first day of your new life, and it is time to start. Pick the lowest-balance account, make it number one, and settle it today.

How to Empower Yourself Financially

(I Did It, and You Can, Too)

Self Financial Empowerment

- I realized that debt had consumed me, so I took charge of all of my finances and strived to live my life debt free (broke my cycle of financial addiction).
- I worked—and you can, too—on debt settlement that resulted in debt elimination.
- I maintained a budget, and it works.
- I stayed ahead with positive thinking that led to positive results.
- I fought hard as a tough-nosed pit-bull negotiator with collection agencies and loan companies and settled for cents on the dollar.
- Once debt was settled, I made a commitment to never fall back into the pit of financial death and bad debt syndrome.
- I tracked bucks. It works and shows you where all your money is being spent (outgoing from your budget).
- I bought a used car instead of a new car. I paid cash and eliminated a high-interest payment, and I owned the car from day one (I put $472 back in my budget every month).
- I eliminated and paid off all cash advances, basically eliminating the legal loan sharks from getting rich off my bad-debt demise (I eliminated 450 percent interest payments on small loans, saving hundreds per month).

- I settled approximately $48,000 in debt for around $11,500 on ten different accounts.
- Wow! I have to pinch myself and say I was bad, but it's finally over today.
- Be supportive to family members during bad-debt times.
- You must realize that once you are debt free, you can—but will not—relapse into financial addiction.
- Share with others, and find ways to help those in financial need once you have a grasp on your own finances. This way, they know they are not alone.
- Buy a copy of this book, and send it to a friend or loved one who is having financial problems.

Just remember, you are not alone, and believe me, I did, and you will, too. You are already reaping the benefits of thousands of saved dollars, and the research has already been done for you by the ways and methods I went through in this process. You are totally taking charge and empowering yourself today. You will also find other methods and things to incorporate into your life by using the methods contained in this book. You will, in the end, defeat the bad-debt enemy.

CHAPTER 11

Financial-Revolution Motivation

With the "Occupy" movements going on globally, it is now more than ever important for each one of us consumers to fight for what we believe in and take a stand. We need to tell ourselves that we are not going to pay higher fees to corporations and financial institutions and allow our elected politicians to spend our hard-earned money. We are not going to let employers engage in unfair labor practices. Yes, we will not stand for or take this at all—period, no exceptions. We the consumers will continue the financial revolution and hold these giant financial corporations accountable for ripping us all off. Yes, we have a choice, and for those unscrupulous companies that engage in these consumer-rip-off schemes, we will not buy from them and support them ever again. We will put the financial noose around *their* necks, and when no one utilizes or purchases from them, we will watch and celebrate these corporate giants going bankrupt. Unscrupulous mortgage companies and loan companies will become nonexistent if we, the small-person consumers, stay strong and stick by one another. Banks will not be able to charge us fees for no reason on ATMs (or whatever the case is), or we will take our money and business elsewhere. Right now, people have left name-brand banks for credit unions, because they typically do not charge these hidden fees.

The bottom line is to keep tracking down your bucks, and establish and maintain that budget we have discussed. Settle your debt, but always do it in a fashion that always benefits you, not the corporations. Do not give up on your Roth IRA or retirement 401(k) plans. Stay with those plans, and watch them grow with time. If you have not set up a retirement, do it right now. Remember, you are your best financial keeper with your own money, so always keep that in mind. Never assume someone else will be as good as you would be, in the end.

Motivational Tools To Use

- Do not say you cannot succeed financially when you *can* and *will.*
- Be honest, especially with yourself and your family.
- As you pay down debt, hope and inspiration start to come when burdensome debt goes away.
- With debt reduction, say, “I am my own person.”
- Reward yourself when properly following your budget.
- Make banks and financial institutions work for you, not you for them.
- Always live within your means.
- Manage budget around a debt-free lifestyle.
- Never recreate debt that is paid off.
- When you wake up every morning, say to yourself, “I am in control, not my creditor.” Today is the beginning of your debt-free life.
- Say, “Today is going to be a great day for my family and me.” (Live it and breathe it.)

Again, understand that hope and change will start to occur right away. Credit scores take time to improve. So stay hopeful, take action, work hard, and fight back to control your own financial future. You can be—and are—your best financial manager with your own money, and with knowledge comes power.

CHAPTER 12

Remedies for Home Loans

What to Do if a Home Loan Gets Denied Due to a Low Credit Score and the Measures to Take

- Get the name of the credit bureau that the lender used that denied your loan.
- Contact the credit bureau and obtain the credit history that they used to determine your score.
- Call the creditor that denied you and ask for exact reasons.
- If not resolved, then dispute the matter using either the online dispute-form process or by writing a letter to the credit bureau disputing the matter.
- You will have to wait for around thirty to forty-five days after the dispute to get the credit bureau to respond.
- After waiting the thirty to forty-five days and clearing the disputed item, you will be able to try again.
- Once the delinquent account is removed, pull credit again and try and get loan approval again.
- Do not give up, and stay on the credit bureaus to do their jobs, as they always work at a snail's pace.

This can be very frustrating, and I know this from personal experience. In this very strict loan-approval economy market, those with the most patience and perseverance prevail. So put on your patience hat when attempting to get a home-loan approval. My wife and I went through five mortgage companies before finally getting our prequalification letter from our lender. I thought that day would never come, but it did for us, and it will for you, too, if you hang in there and do what they ask you to do to make the loan go through. We used a direct lender, but that choice is always up to you as a family or individual. There are many lenders out there, so shop around, and pick the one that you feel the most comfortable with in the end. I recommend the direct lender because the savings are enormous in the end. Always look at the Better Business Bureau in their state and area to make sure they do not have reputability issues or problems. Always check out past customers' comments on their company's reviews online. I measure my lender by if they have an A rating or not, which is also a good idea. This means they have a proven track record as a lender.

What remedy do I have if a credit bureau does not remove the delinquent account after the creditor has removed it?

- Write a letter demanding the item be removed from your credit report and that your score reflects the change.
- You can threaten to take legal action against them under the Fair Credit Reporting Act.
- Pay an attorney to write a demand letter to the credit bureau and, if needed, file suit against them. (Usually they will assist once an attorney is involved).
- Have your attorney sue them and demand attorney's fees and damages for you.

What do I do when I get my pre-approval home-loan letter from the lender?

- Start a "favorite" list of the homes you like the best. I recommend the top five.
- Drive by each home, and if you do not like the home or the neighborhood, then shrink the list down to your top three.

- Driving around the neighborhood after dark may even give you a better idea as to what kind of neighborhood it really is; at night, it shows its true colors.
- Contact your real estate agent and see inside the top three homes.
- Pick the most favored house, and make an offer through your real estate agent.

I always tell people: when looking for a home, take your time. Do not take the matter lightly or be pressured by anyone. Try and get the most square footage and lot space for your money, if possible. Always have your agent make the offer contingent upon the home passing the home inspection, and never buy the home without paying for a home inspection. The inspection could save you from buying a money pit that could even bankrupt you in the end. Home inspections reveal any hidden problems, and those you want to know about before finalizing the deal.

I talked with a friend of mine who is a past financial-mortgage specialist. My friend let me know that the reason for getting out of the industry was due to the problems that prime lenders got into giving out high-interest loans when they knew people could not pay them back (quite a few years ago), and they got into trouble with the savings-and-loans issues. My friend does stand by the fact that real estate cycles, and today's homeowners should just hang onto their properties, because in two to five years, they will be able to probably double their money. So if you own a home, do not stop on your home-improvement projects; now is the time to improve to sell later. Presently, it's a buyer's market so if you are hunting for a home, now is the time to buy one.

Do not forget that you do not ever want to take on more than you can afford in a home loan. Presently, people are losing their homes due to foreclosure and short sales, because they initially took on too high of a mortgage payment and overextended themselves. You can buy a short sale and get into a really sweet deal, but if you make the same errors as the previous owner, you could be the one losing the home next—so always keep that in mind when purchasing.

This is why it is important to be debt free. It's vital to have savings, when buying a home, to have as a safety net. You never know: if a crisis occurs, you do not want to lose your home. I recommend having at least a one-year house-payment reserve, and if something major happens, you have a year to get back on track. This way, you will not be foreclosed on and lose your dream house.

Pointers when buying a home

- Take your time and enjoy the process.
- Improve your credit score and get the best interest rates possible.
- Make sure you have little debt to the highest income you can show on paper to your lender when getting a loan approved.
- Have your real estate agent/broker do a property analysis, and always do a home inspection.
- Make sure the home has good electrical, plumbing, roofing, and no mold, no termites, or major water damage.
- Do not worry about upgrading the home, as you can paint yourself and hire a contractor to do a lot of the upgrades over a period of time. Sometimes without all the upgrades, you can get a better price on the home, meaning a lower mortgage payment. Granite countertops and other upgrades can come when you are able to afford them at a later time.
- Do not worry about appliances coming with the home. I always buy new ones, as I want my own, anyway, and not someone else's hand-me-down refrigerator or washing machine.

CHAPTER 13

Moving into Your New House

Well, you have finally done it—purchased your new home. You have made one of the single hardest and best purchases of your entire life for your and your family's future. During this process, you have also improved your credit score to be able to buy the house of your dreams. You have a set budget now, and by budgeting, you will be able to afford making some upgrades and improvements on your home. You will not be house poor, because your mortgage payment will be in line with your budget and what you are able to afford to prevent foreclosure in the future. Below, I have listed some move-in tips for you when making the move to your new home.

Home Move-In Tips

- Find an affordable mover to help you with the move. (Get three bids and then pick the one you like the best.)
- Move as many smaller items as you can before hiring the mover; this will cut down on some of the moving cost.
- Paint any major room color changes and schemes before moving in. There is nothing worse than smelling paint fumes and knocking into freshly painted walls—or having a painting-project mess while living in the home. So paint first, move in second.
- Major construction projects, if you can afford to, do prior to moving in, as well.
- Do not go crazy and buy all-new furniture, appliances, and so on. I buy a few new pieces each pay period when I can afford them.

- Do all major cleaning of the house before moving in; if you have to, hire a maid to do a professional cleaning, and if the carpets are in need, always have them professionally steam cleaned before moving into the home.
- Move in and be happy in your nice, freshly cleaned, and newly painted home. Yes, it's new because you placed your own stamp on the house before moving into it.

The final move will always have some snags, so don't get stressed out. Make sure that you give a thirty-day notice to your old landlord prior to the move and close of escrow on your home purchase. Make sure you get your deposit from your old landlord after moving out. Enjoy the new-home moving process, and try not to get upset and stress over the move. Remember, once you move into the home, it's your home and safe haven. Do not forget that during the move-in process. You are now living the American dream of home ownership.

CHAPTER 14

Financial Philosophies

I want to pound something into your head: this is to always have a budget. Always follow that budget, track your bucks, and be persistent when dealing with creditors and credit bureaus. Pay off and settle outstanding debts for as low as possible. If you have to and credit bureaus or creditors push you too hard, then sue them, but only as a last resort.

When purchasing a home, do not forget to use programs like VA, FHA, USDA, and other loan programs out there. USDA loans typically require you to pay a down payment of 3.5 percent of the home or closing costs (or both). VA loans are usually zero money down if you are a qualified veteran. Remember, VA loans and USDA usually have minimum credit scores ranging from 620–640. Most lenders, of course, like the highest credit score you can qualify with, as safeguard to themselves.

After purchasing the home, hire a reasonable moving company with the best customer reviews, and hire a cleaning service to clean your home and make it new.

I am going to change the subject here a little and let each and every one of you new homebuyers or prospective buyers know that I am going to change the credit laws in this great nation. I am tired of politicians, credit bureaus, creditors, collection agencies, and financial giants controlling us as consumers and bleeding us dry financially. These financial giants must be held accountable for their actions. I like the Occupy movements globally, because they are making a difference, and I support them in full. We the people are not going to—and do not have to—take their rip-off tactics any more, and with social media, they are becoming exposed every day. We do not have to pay fees that we see as not acceptable or just plain unfair, and we do not have to do business with these companies that rip off the little consumer. The bottom line here is that we the consumers do not have to take their crap any more, and we will not be pushed around. While the rich get richer paying less in taxes, the poor get poorer covering those higher taxes, and, in drastic cases, the poor fall off into homelessness, not being able to keep up with society any more.

I will also encourage all my readers, as a major tip, to always read fine print with any business transaction—and especially with home loans or car loans. If you do not, these hidden fees can light your pocketbook on fire, and you can end up payer higher interest rates, higher payments, and fees for items that you do not even know why you are paying them. Be a smart consumer; knowledge is power, so question anything that you are concerned about, and make that lender explain why you have to pay that fee. Question all aspects of any loan that you take out before ever signing for ownership of that loan. Once you sign, then the problem becomes yours.

It is time for all of us consumers to take a stand in a peaceful but assertive fashion. We need to protest against those corrupt financial corporate giants, those unscrupulous employers, and financial-fee corruption; and together, along with social media, we can and will make a difference. Yes, we the people—through Occupy movements and not conducting business and engaging in services with these unscrupulous business—will watch them crumble at our fingertips; and, most of all, through our togetherness and teamwork as smart, honest consumers who have knowledge, we will be powerful once and for all. Those politicians that do not follow our interests will be voted out by us in the next election and replaced with those politicians that look after us—the consumers and voters that elect them to work for all of us, not *us* for *them*. Together, we will stand, and they will work with us, or we will make them fail. The people have spoken, and we are calling them out; and if they misbehave, we are voting them off the island and taking them to the woodshed for their punishment. In this game of life, those who team up for honesty will eliminate those who are dishonest and unscrupulous and expose them for those horrific types of practices. Yes, if we have to, we will sue those corporations that take advantage of us and rip us all off, in order to recoup our own damages against them. Now is the time to take action.

CHAPTER 15

Taking Out a Car Loan

I am devoting this chapter to taking out car loans. Whether it is a used car or a new one, you still, as a consumer, need to be aware of sales tactics or gimmicks that can cost you a bundle.

First of all, you never want to overextend yourself or let any sales manager or salesman talk you into a car that you cannot afford. Watch out for their smooth talking, read the fine print, and get bottom-line answers when working out the loan. Loan shopping prior to buying the car can save you bundles. Below are some loan-shopping tips.

Loan-Shopping Tips

- Based on your FICO score, shop around for the lowest-possible interest rate. Usually a credit union is your best place to shop at.
- Never take out a poor-credit or high-interest loan. It's better to wait until your credit score can get you a good rate.
- Never go over 11 percent on any car loan, or you will regret it in the end.
- Get three loan quotes from three different companies. Online, you have endless resources and companies to choose from for a car loan.
- Seek out a car loan from 2.49 to 9.9 percent interest to keep your payments in your budget.
- Always shop for a car you can afford; never go over what your budget will handle.
- Do not buy a $30,000 car if you can only afford a $15,000 one; doing so only helps the salesman and screws you over.

- Shop at least three car dealerships and compare prices, go with the lower-priced car, and use your already-approved loan financing. Never do the financing through the dealership, as they will charge you bucket loads of money with their high-interest loan companies that will finance you and rip you off.
- Make car dealerships fight for your business, and let them know you know what the car is worth. Look on *Kelley Blue Book*; it tells you what that year of car is worth.
- I recommend using a credit union for financing 100 percent of the time.
- Have a family member go with you, and ask for their opinion before buying the car. A second opinion from a friend or relative can save you from making the wrong costly decision on a car sale.
- I recommend buying a used car with lower mileage than a brand new car.
- If possible, pay cash; this saves you interest completely, as there is no loan, and you own the car the minute you drive it off the lot.

Positives to Purchasing a Used Car

- You pay less for the car, usually.
- There are lower payments.
- Some cars are reasonable enough that you can buy the used car with cash and have no payment.
- Car dealers will negotiate prices more loosely, as they want to sell them off their lot.
- Always have a mechanic check out the used car prior to the final purchase, even if you have to pay a fee for the mechanic to do so. Do this 100 percent of the time.

Tips for Buying a New Car

- Shop within your financial means and budget 100 percent of the time.
- Only purchase when the car is on sale or has a large rebate.
- Get approval at a credit union, and buy the car with a low-interest car loan.
- Always negotiate the sticker price on the vehicle with the salesman and finance manager. Typically, they will come down $2,000 to $5,000 off the sticker price.
- Watch for higher sticker prices from a lot of dealerships, as they will try and use that against you, saying they have *already* come down in their prices; in actuality, you just paid more for the car.
- Internet car-dealership departments even offer lower prices if you find the car online, in some cases.
- Compare prices between dealerships online and then go into the lower dealership.
- Take your time and test-drive a lot of different cars. I recommend taking thirty to ninety days to find the right car.
- Typically during the months of October, November, and December—at the end of the year—a lot of dealerships want to sell cars in order to get new inventory and can work out great deals during their end-of-the-year sales.
- Good luck, and make the best decision with the best payment and interest rate.

Sales Danger Signs When Buying Either a New or Used Car

- Don't be lured into paying more for the car than it is worth.
- Before buying a used car, get a full-engine-diagnostic check performed by an ASC-certified mechanic.

- Inspect the vehicle before driving it off the lot.
- Always negotiate the sticker price of car, whether it is used or new.
- Save up so that you can put a nice comfortable down payment on the car to keep your payment and interest down.
- Get a credit union lower-interest loan.
- Call your insurance company to make sure your car insurance will not be too high and out of your budget.
- Always take a friend or family member that can talk sense into you so you do not overspend or buy a car that is not right for you and your family.
- Second opinions work, even if you have to call someone to get it when buying the car.
- Read the contract from start to finish, and *all* fine print, making sure there are no hidden fees; ask questions if in doubt.
- Good luck on your next car purchase!

Please do not forget the principles you have been taught. A car and a home are two of the largest purchases you may ever make in your life. These purchase are rewarding if done the right and educated way. The wrong purchase can drain you financially and can have a major impact if out of budget—and can even bankrupt you in the end. Be smart and keep tracking down those bucks that are being spent.

The best way to buy a car is to compare prices online through a search engine on your computer. I usually check out all used and new dealerships, and then I call them to make sure the cars are there before I ever visit the dealership. Test-driving every vehicle is mandatory; never buy before driving it. In the end, keep all loan documents in a filing cabinet where they are safe and secure. Now enjoy the new luxury of car and home ownership.

CHAPTER 16

Motivational Financial Tools

This chapter is a motivational tool to remind you, if you are not carefully financially, where you could end up. If you are not diligent with your finances, you can end up homeless.

I interviewed several transients (homeless people), and they all had a pattern of behavior. The pattern was that most of the homeless had traumatic and tragic stories of life-changing events that took place in their individual lives. A lot even suffered from mental illness and drug addiction. Most talked about how they used to work and be productive, law-abiding citizens prior to their life-changing event or events. Others shared about how hard economic times took a spiral effect on their lives. Some expressed how they literally went from riches to rags.

I would say, as a rough estimate, that around 75 percent of the transients I spoke to stated something to the effect of, "drugs and alcohol snowballed on me." They attributed their usage to being stressed out financially and/or as a result of employment loss. The two usually went hand in hand. Again, I want to say that all or most talked about how debt plagued them, and they just gave into it and gave up and fell into homelessness. Others stated, "I was hanging on barely and still had a place to live, but when my boss laid me off or fired me for being late to work, I just snapped and became homeless almost overnight. I had no way to pay my bills, collectors, car payments, rent, or mortgage—or even feed myself." However, to my surprise, almost 60 percent of those I communicated with stated having a plan to get out of their homeless situation if given the right opportunity again. Approximately 40 percent of those I communicated with had pretty much given in, and homelessness seemed to be their new way of existence. A lot were already receiving some sort of government subsidy, either Medi-Cal, Medicare, SSI disability, food stamps, or indigent stipends and were going from shelter to shelter and program to program just to survive.

This needs to be a lesson to all of us when we go out and buy expensive new motorcycles, boats, RVs, computers, new cell phones, video games, expensive shoes, clothing, new cars, or new homes, especially when we cannot afford them. There are a lot of things I did not mention, and believe me, they could take up an entire book if listed. Guess what—this is all just *stuff.* Stuff is basically things we can live without. Many of the homeless I described above were people just like us, with lots of stuff, and when the economy hit rock bottom, they lost their stuff just like *you* can; and you can become them if you are not careful.

So, people, financially, let's wake up, smell the java, and get real in life. I will give you a true story. In 2011, my car was totaled in a rear-end collision. My car payment at the time was $472 per month and had a very-high-interest loan on it. At the time of the accident, I had paid on the car for almost sixty months, and it still had two payments left on it. After the accident, it was basically worth nothing, and I got hardly any money for it from my insurance company. I was the victim, and I was not at fault. This car had been a $22,000 car brand new. I received around $3,800 for it. Now keep in mind, this was only fifty-eight months since the original purchase. So, as you can see a car, is a very poor investment. I ended up paying cash for an older car, and I am still driving it today; I have no loan, no payments, and I own the car outright. So now, with no car payment, I am saving $472 per month. We have to be diligent with our finances as times are hard.

I am not trying to scare you to death, but a lot of us consumers are one paycheck away from joining the homeless. Yes, they are real people just like all of us. We need to cut down and watch what we are doing and start tracking those bucks in our budgets right now—before it's too late.

It *is* okay to budget in a movie, dinner out, or even that needed used car or home. What I am saying is to avoid the stuff you do not need for survivability. Trust me, not having lots of stuff means not having those bills, and to me, quality of life is way better than stuff.

Problems with some employers in these poor financial times

- They don't value their workers.
- Some do not give legal meal and rest periods, deny employees ten-minute breaks, deny thirty-minute lunches, and make employees sign documents stating they are complying with policies when they are not and never plan to be following their own policies and procedures.
- I recommend to employees to sue your employer if they are doing the above.
- Any employer violation of the labor code, sue them big time.
- Corporations are not giving raises, and cost of living is increasing.
- Employers are, in a sense, threatening employees by stating, "There are thousands of workers out there that would take your job in a second if you don't perform."
- Employers are replacing employees that get injured while they are out on medical leave.
- Employers are not accommodating employees that are disabled or have other disabilities.
- Employers are not following the labor laws and FMLA (Family Medical Leave Act) laws.
- Employers in this economy have the "bigger than life" complex. Take them down by a lawsuit if they violate the law.
- Employers are eliminating full-time positions to part-time positions to cut out and prevent employees from getting benefits that they need for themselves and family members.

Believe me, I could list twenty more items above, but this book would be five hundred pages long. So I will keep this simple and bottom-line it. Does the employee have rights in this age of economic crisis? What are the action steps the employee can take? See below for the five action steps an employee can take if this is occurring.

Five Employee Action Steps

- Contact an attorney and get legal advice on the matter at hand.
- You can file a complaint yourself online with DFEH (Department of Fair Employment and Housing).
- You can go right to a lawsuit with an attorney once you get a right-to-sue letter from DFEH.
- Keep a daily journal documenting all labor-law violations from your employer, document if you are denied lunch or breaks, also write down in the journal other employees that can be witnesses at a later date.
- E-mail your supervisor and request that they relieve you for breaks and lunches, and when they refuse in the e-mail, copy it and save it as a future legal document against your employer.

Always remember: you do have rights as an employee. Most companies do not want employees to really know their rights. Employers want their employees to be uneducated to all of their rights. Employers can and will be fined for violations of the state labor codes. State labor agencies are watchdogs over employers, and so is the federal government's EEOC (Equal Opportunity Employment Commission). You can sue your employer any time you are their victim and they violate the labor code. In fact, most companies will not go to court, because they know they will lose. Think about it: jurors are people just like us, and they would love to award hundreds, thousands, or, if given the opportunity, *millions* to a victimized employee. The majority of the time, in fear of losing, employers will settle their lawsuits before ever going to court once the formal lawsuit is filed. Corporations and other private companies have or retain attorneys, and they never want a lawsuit published, so 95 percent of the time, they will try and work out a settlement with the employee plaintiff to make the matter go away once and for all. They do not want other employees to know about it, so they make them sign agreements not to discuss the terms of the settlement with anyone.

I am a firm believer that if or when an employer tries to unlawfully terminate an employee, that employee should seek legal counsel and sue that employer 100 percent of the time. This would put the fear of God in all employers nationwide, and they may stop trying to screw over so many people in this fashion. Believe me: when they unlawfully terminate you, they are screwing you over, so you have nothing to lose by suing them for their law violation—only something to gain.

So the next time a human-resource manager tries to scare you with the "you are dispensable" routine or "you are an at-will employee, and we can get rid of you at any time," this is the wrong answer on their part, and you can and *should* sue them big time to prevent them from doing this to someone else. Labor-law violations have to be stopped by an employee immediately.

Financially, you can and should revolt and make them pay for their negative actions. The only thing that "at will" means is that you as an employee can quit and walk away from your employer any time you want to do it. Some employers will try to get tricky and lay you off and state that it's due to company downsizing. This is okay as an employee. When you get laid off, congrats—you can collect unemployment, and consider this your paid vacation. I will encourage you to actively seek out new employment, but you will be compensated until that occurs.

A good rule of thumb with labor law is to consult with a labor-law specialist. These attorneys deal with these legal matters on a daily basis and, in most cases, will offer you one free consultation. During your initial consultation, you will be able to discuss with the attorney your case, and they will decide if they think you will win if the matter goes to court. I recommend if an attorney tells you in the consultation that you do not have a case or it is too weak to pursue, then do not waste your time; move on and seek new employment with a much better and reputable company.

However, on the flip side, if you are told you have a case after your initial consultation, then let the attorney represent you, and take that employer all the way to the bank. Some attorney's may even offer to do a class-action case for you, and other employees that have been screwed will also benefit. I recommend doing it if you have the chance. This may help others in the long run and make the bad employers clean up their act and stop discriminating against their employees. Usually, the class-action attorney will take your case on a contingency basis, meaning if you do not win, they do not get paid. The percentage from this type of attorney is usually that you get 60 percent and they get 40 percent upon winning the lawsuit. It's fair trade, because without the attorney, you would get nothing, anyway.

CHAPTER 17

Timeshares

One of the first methods of downsizing for your retirement is to get rid of your timeshare. This is very cost efficient and should be first on your list to get rid of. Thousands of people globally have suffered from purchasing a timeshare. A timeshare, in my opinion, is by far one of the biggest mistakes a person could ever make financially. I will point out some major reasons why this is true. I personally can tell you this because I used to own one myself.

First of all, most of this timeshare places are in resorts. The timeshare companies are strictly out to "resort" you out of your money. They put on these vacation facades to lure people into buying them. These huge timeshare corporations are legally going to rip you off when you buy one. They will tell you that when you buy it, you can use it any time. This is where the lies begin: during the timeshare presentation. The salesperson will offer you everything under the sun just to get you to sign away your hard-earned cash so that they can make a large commission. I can tell you that every time I wanted to use my timeshare, they were booked solid and there was no reservation available. I had to use the resort when it was not even convenient for me to take a vacation during that time of the year. The salespeople, of course, leave that detail out. Then every month I was paying around $170, and I was not even using the timeshare, because I had to work to pay on it. I never was able to get a reservation during my vacation times, so it was not even of any use to my family or me. So I spent around $2,040 per year on my monthly ownership fees. I owned the timeshare for six years, and I estimate I lost around $14,640 on a timeshare I could barely use (four times in six years). I had to go to the same location, because everywhere else would have required me to spend money on air flight, which was exorbitant at the time. So the sales pitch about flying to paradises was not my reality. That much money could have been a nice down payment on a house, or I could have paid cash for a car. Better than that, if I had put the $14,640 in a Roth IRA, I would have it for my retirement right now. The story gets even worse, though: when my ex-wife and I divorced, she took it away from me, and it was listed in the Marital Settlement Agreement as her sole and separate property. Still worse, she used it and burned all the vacation points up and then refused to pay any payments on it. So *then* what happened was that the timeshare company sent this to collection. They still came after me for payment, because I had purchased the timeshare with my ex-wife, and we signed a contract with them together; they did not acknowledge the Marital Settlement Agreement. This is where my real nightmare began. I explained that I was not legally responsible, and they told me they would foreclose and wreck my credit if I did not pay them. The Marital Settlement Agreement was not worth the paper it was written on in this case. I ended up having to settle with the timeshare company's collection agency for $3,350 in a deed-in-lieu settlement. In essence, I paid $3,350 to *give them back* the timeshare. My nightmare was just beginning with them. Even after that, I had to hire an attorney and locate my ex-wife to get her notarized signature until they would take the delinquencies off my credit report.

Do not buy a timeshare! They will only cause you problems. I got totally hammered with the purchase of my timeshare. In the end, I paid $17,990 for something that I had to give back to the timeshare company so they could rip someone else off with the same legal scam. My credit got ruined over this entire ordeal, and I got virtually only bills out of my timeshare. I have talked to others, and about eight out of ten people I have talked to have had similar experiences with timeshare ownership. Most of us wish we had never gotten involved with the timeshare company. It was the most costly mistake I ever have made in my life, and I would never do it again. Buy *real* property that you can use anytime you want and *when* you want.

In my opinion, timeshares are legal Ponzi schemes. These unscrupulous companies will drain you dry financially if you buy into the scam. So do not be fooled by their free timeshare-retreat seminars or free vacation getaways. They are all rip-off artists waiting to convince you to be scammed into buying a timeshare. The old adage "nothing is free" applies to timeshares.

Timeshare companies will tell you in their sales pitches that you can rent them out like owning an apartment; this is a myth. They will also tell you that a timeshare is easy to sell, like a house purchase. This is another myth, as there are companies out there advertising that they sell time shares, but they charge high fees and never guarantee, after taking your up-front fees, even selling the time share. So, no; they are not easy to sell. In my opinion, buying a timeshare is like throwing your money away and flushing it down a toilet with absolutely no return in the end. Plus, if you ever pay your timeshare payment late, the company will ban you from using it until it is paid up. Another factor is that a lot of timeshare companies charge maintenance fees every ninety, days and they can be around $150 to $200. I read an article about a man who lost his timeshare because the company did a new renovation, and he could not pay the timeshare owner's $1,500 renovation fee. It ruined his credit, and he lost the timeshare after owning it for approximately twelve years. Terrible story, but this is a regular occurrence when dealing with a timeshare. If you own one right now, try to do a deed-in-lieu and get out from underneath it—if the timeshare company will even do one with you in this depressed economic market. If they will not, you basically are in trouble in the long run, and good luck in paying fee after fee and not owning anything in the end. Hopefully, after reading this section, you will never make this poor purchase.

I do recommend saving your hard-earned cash and going on a cash-paid vacation. This way, you can choose where to go and when you want to go, and by making vacation reservations, you are on your way to a nice, relaxing break from everyday stress and work. Try and plan at least two trips per year when retired. When preparing for retirement, plan at least one major vacation trip every year, and save up for it in advance. This way, you can really relax knowing that it is already paid for and that you will not have overspent or maxed out your individual credit cards to where you will have to pay on the vacation throughout the year. I recommend having a vacation fund, much like the concept of a savings account. Also, become a member of AAA (American Automobile Association), as they have great travel packages and give special discounts to members.

Remember: plan ahead for your vacation, budget the money, and I wish everyone a safe and affordable vacation.

Preparing your financial future

So far, we have discussed the importance of having a retirement plan. If you do not have a 401(k), 403(b), or SEP, then see if your employer offers any one of these programs. Typically, most employers offer 401(k) plans, and if they have matching funds, then this is free money, and sign up immediately for your 401(k).

Now, if you have no retirement option through your employer, which is starting to become the norm with employers, then start your retirement future with a Roth IRA. I personally feel it is the best individual retirement plan, but, if in doubt, seek the advice of a certified financial advisor to assist you with your retirement plan.

Rule number one: never take money out of a retirement IRA or plan. There are strict penalties for taking money out, and you run the risk of never replacing it and not having a retirement plan when the time comes. So just do not do it—period. At the end of the book, the financial advisor I interviewed will go into this more in depth and will talk about how much to contribute into your retirement account.

Ideas of action as an employee

In this day of economic uncertainty, if you lose your job, you are at risk of losing everything, and there will not be any retirement for you in the end. We the consumers continue to be used by politicians for their political agendas, and the rich get richer paying less in taxes and making millions of dollars. Some companies are called "private equity firms," and they buy struggling companies, drain all their assets, and then run off with the money. This is basically a legal way to steal from and bankrupt a company. We have people running for presidential offices that have done just that for employment. I do not know about you, but I would never vote for someone like that—especially not for President of the United States.

So we need to protect our retirement plans (401(k) or 403(b)). If you as an employee are retaliated against or fired for no reason, seek professional legal advice immediately, and treat your employment and retirement like your own business. Taking action may even prevent other employees from losing their retirement plans. In my opinion, fight fire with fire to save your hard-earned retirement plan. Companies have attorneys; so get your own to save your future assets.

If you currently work for a good employer that has a good 401(k) matching fund, then stay with them, as they are the minority in the nation. Take advantage of any opportunity they offer, and if they have profit-sharing SEP, then you are way ahead of the retirement game, and you, my friend, are going to have a very lucrative retirement future. Good luck! Plan ahead and retire stress and debt free.

There are great retirement plans out there. Some major companies that have proven records are three top companies, T. Rowe Price, Vanguard, and Fidelity (not listed in any order). In my opinion, stay away from companies that do not have proven track records, as you do not want to lose everything in a Ponzi scheme when they run off with your money, and you are conned out of your retirement. Believe me, this happens more regularly than we want to think about. The big three companies above have no reported problems, and lots of people are making money on their retirement plans through these big three. Reputability is everything with retirement investing.

Retirement Ideas

- Purchase your own home with a thirty-year, fixed-rate loan at the lowest possible interest you can lock the loan in with.
- Budget your mortgage payment, and never buy a home out of your budget.
- Live within your financial means daily, weekly, monthly, and yearly.
- Do not support adult children, or some may spend your retirement. Do not enable them; you can help slightly, but make them accountable for their own bills and rents.
- Save up and pay cash for vacations, and budget them into your budget always.
- Don't buy stuff you do not need. Vanity will put you in the poor house over time.
- Pay off debt, and place some of that extra monthly income into your Roth IRA.
- Limit eating out and coffee out. Indulge in this as a reward for following your budget.
- Avoid unnecessary travel costs. If you live close enough to town, run errands by walking them or riding a bike to save cash on gasoline.

These are only a few tips, and, believe me, there are a lot more out there to assist you in the long haul.

Downsizing for Retirement

We have already covered downsizing and getting rid of play toys, boats, motorcycles, RVs, and so on; so let's explore the idea of downsizing from a large house to a smaller one to save money in your budget. A lot of elderly are currently getting advice to do this, because the smaller the property and less expensive, the cheaper the property taxes. Also, having a smaller yard to maintain is a big help to some. Some retirees even go into condominiums with no yard to have to worry about. These are all great ideas that will save you money when you're nearing retirement or when you are getting close to getting your gold watch.

What to do if you fall into this category? Very simple: sell your old, large home and use the money to downsize to the more affordable house. This usually will also give you an extra cash reserve, because you will profit off the sale of the house and have money left over after buying the cheaper property with low maintenance.

Also, I will encourage all people now at or close to retirement age to get a will in place to protect your assets from being given away to the state where you live. If your spouse is not listed as a beneficiary, then do so on all your financial accounts and mortgage. This way, if one of you has an accident or dies all of a sudden, the other will be taken care of and will not lose their financial security and home. I recommend for everyone to get a life-insurance policy. None of us can control our own destiny. I hear people say all the time, "I will do it tomorrow." Well, guess what—tomorrow may not come, so don't procrastinate; get your finances in order today, or it may be too late.

Results of My Interview with a Financial Advisor That Will Help You Enormously with Your Finances

I was fortunate enough to be able to interview a very well-respected and professional certified financial advisor in the city of San Luis Obispo, California. The financial advisor educated me a lot about what a financial advisor does.

So do you know what a certified financial advisor does? No? Okay, here it is: a financial advisor performs many duties in helping to direct client's financial decisions. These can be individual and/or business financial advising. The advisor will do this so his clients will achieve good decisions in improving their wealth and/or getting out of debt. The financial advisor can also focus on assisting the client with retirement planning and programs available to them. Financial advisors help their clients improve financially—based upon the clients' needs—and desire to help them succeed.

The financial advisor let me know that having a budget is vital to a client's financial success. By the financial advisor getting all his client's financial details together, the advisor is able to make better headway when planning his client's final retirement plan. This also holds true in preparing for a client to buy a house, buy a car, go to college, or send children to college.

The advisor went on to say that if you are a person in debt, he/she will take you and correct that habit so that when the debt is paid off and corrected, you do not fall *back* into debt. The financial advisor called this "the cooling-off period of purchases." Financial advisors, in some extreme cases, will even advise their clients to cut up and destroy all credit cards. They will advise the clients to do this so they are not tempted to use them and fall back into their spending habits. Sometimes a financial advisor may even advise a client to truffle credit cards from the highest to the lowest interest rate and destroy the highest-interest-rate credit card. This is a form of credit-card consolidation, and it has been proven to work in some individual cases. The financial advisor I interviewed said, "Today, we do not do this much, because there are not that many companies out there that will offer low or even zero interest on their credit cards. I believe those days have been long gone." Plus, the advisor recommends, if possible, to always pay off the one credit card you have for emergencies at the end of every month; it can improve your FICO score, which also lets you have a higher balance available for an emergency if one occurs.

When we discussed tracking your bucks, the financial advisor was very specific. Currently, a lot of people lose track of money, especially cash, when using their ATM cards. The advisor mentioned that clients often spend large sums of money every day on eating out lunches and on morning coffee. So these are some areas to be very conscientious about when trying to save and track down your expenditures.

This financial advisor stated, "A Roth IRA is an excellent vehicle for retirement options." He also recommends to those people over fifty years of age to max out, if they can afford it, the maximum yearly contribution of $6,000 (and if under age fifty, the maximum is $5,000 for the Roth IRA). If you have a 401(k), a 403(b), or an SEP (Simplified Employee Pension) available through your place of employment, the financial advisor recommends to take advantage of any program where you get profit sharing (as in an SEP or matched funds in some 401(k) or 403(b) programs). Matching funds from an employer, according to the financial advisor, is almost like getting free money, with you only having to put up a little to receive those matching funds. So the advisor said, "In matching funds, max them out so you are getting double the money, so it is free money, when you think about." This is the "magic" associated with matching funds, which will help you get your retirement rolling in full force.

I asked about home and car purchases. The financial advisor said, "Buying a home is a place to live as in a shelter. Buying rental property can be considered a good investment property. Yes, you can, on some occasions, make money on the sale of a home, but just consider your house as your place to live and enjoy some tax breaks associated with home ownership. On the other hand, a car is the worst purchase that you will ever make, but we need cars to travel, so you have to have one, for the most part." The advisor recommends that you "purchase a used vehicle with low mileage, usually two to three years old, as they are in better shape and more mechanically sound, usually. There are some exceptions, but a car two to three years old, in most cases, is pretty new and solid mechanically."

So you have heard it from the certified professional financial advisor. You have gained knowledge and power by reading this book. You now have a solid foundation for becoming debt free; use this book as an indispensable tool in your financial toolbox in order to fix your financial future and become your own financial manager in years to come.

Good luck in becoming debt free, and remember: once you are free and liberated from debt, never relapse and return to the bad-credit pit of financial death. Stay positive, take action now, and look ahead. With hard work, determination, patience, perseverance, and motivation—along with positive thinking—you will succeed financially.

Made in the USA
Monee, IL
04 November 2026

67377445R00056